RAW

One Woman's Journey Through Love, Loss, and Cancer

Fiona Finn

ISBN: 1492129933
ISBN 13: 9781492129936

Acknowledgments

Since I can't say THANK YOU enough, I will try to say it in as many different languages as possible. First and foremost, thank you, God, for saving me from myself. *Muchas gracias!*

Mindfully, I thank my parents, Michael and Christina Burke, for a lifetime of love and sacrifice. *Merci beaucoup!*

My children, Ryan, Connor, and Nieve, I thank you for just being. I love you each unconditionally. *Grazie mille!*

Without a late-night chat over wine with Catherine and Derville Quigley, this book would never have been written. *Go raibh maith agat!*

I may never be able to fully thank my sister, Deirdre Hanley, for giving me and my children shelter when no one else would. *Spasibo!*

Ia Divens, thank you for being my armchair psychologist, loyal friend, and hair stylist for over a decade. *Domo arigato!*

I just have to give a huge shout out to Shine Hair Studio for hosting a benefit for me and my children during my fight against colon cancer. *Teşekkür ederim!*

Where would I be if my auntie, Patricia O'Gorman, hadn't loved and supported me during the most painful ordeal in my life? *Danke!*

To my truly great friends who were hard to find, difficult to leave, and impossible to forget—Angie Shaudys, Bridgid Whitford, Dawn Plate, Jack Allen, Jennifer Evans, Fatima Boucinha and Neil Kagan. *Obrigado!*

Honestly, thank you Sharon Robinson for encouraging me to speak my truth. *Tak!*

Honorable mentions must go out to Michelle Meleo with www.mindtripproductions.com for designing the cover of *Raw* and Jeff & Dodie Jodice with Inspired Images for their photography. *Kiitos paljon!*

Last but not least, to all those who hurt me, betrayed me, disappointed me, and broke my heart—for this,

I say thank you, wholeheartedly. Your hate, made me stronger, and the fact you left me, showed me nothing lasts forever. *Do je, Efharisto, Sukria, Xie xie, Dêkuji, Mahalo, Tak, Toda, Kamsa hamnida, Takk, Salamat po, Dziekuje, Istutity, Asante, Kawp-kun krap/ka, Cam o, Termi kasih!*

Contents

Preface

No lie, *Raw* has been over two decades in the making. I'll be the first to admit that Aristotle said it best: *"Knowing yourself is the beginning of all wisdom."* And I am no Aristotle. What I am is a housewife and mother, and that role has run from the ordinary to the extraordinary. I used to believe that I knew myself— really knew myself. But when I was faced with a few of life's challenges all at once, I can honestly say I surprised everyone, including myself. I fell apart and landed in a psych ward, unable to compartmentalize what had happened to my so-called life.

Who doesn't want to remember only the fond memories in their lives? I know I do. That being said, it took ages to write this memoir, putting pen to paper or fingers to keyboard. Each time I would sit down to write, fear would set in. Fear that I would have to relive the pain of rejection and abandonment again—this time by choice, during the act of writing. Year after year I would remind myself that if at first you don't succeed, try, try again. Finally, it's done, it's real, and you are reading my life story—pure, simple, and unadulterated.

I promise I've told the whole truth and nothing but the truth. Of course, I had to change a few names to protect the innocent (and not so innocent). Trust me; there is an ex—or two—who would gladly sue my ass if given the opportunity. Defamation is communicating false statements, and I swear in front of God that I am dealing strictly with the truth. If you're going to expose the truth, as I have, then you have to be prepared for upsetting a few people, right? What I have is a story worth telling, so instead of brushing it under the table, I'm serving it on a silver platter, housewife style!

Sure, I've had my share of loss in life—more than some and less than others. Don't we all have our own crosses to bear? I can't tell you how many people hit me with the comment "you're so strong" during my life's low points. But I didn't want to be any fucking stronger. Sorry about the cursing, but I want to be honest with you, and in my life, when I feel it necessary, I curse. I didn't want to be stronger; I wanted to be loved. When I finally accepted my past, I began to understand that the experience of love is both a blessing and curse.

You may have wondered, what's up with the bleeding onion on the cover? Well, the process of writing *Raw* was like skinning an onion, so much so I bled. Each layer of myself I peeled back, I discovered another inner layer even more fearful of being vulnerable. As kids, we believed that as soon as we became adults we would no longer be vulnerable. But soon we learn that one never outgrows vulnerability. It took some time, but finally I realized that if *Raw* was to be really raw and uncut, then I would have to leave everything on the table for you, my readers. So, dinner's ready. Come and eat, for I'm serving up some food for your soul.

Chapter 1:

DISARMED

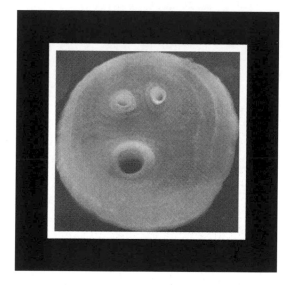

"I like it when the deeper you go with the character, the more you see the layers start to peel away."
—Edward Norton

I had just returned to sunny southwest Florida for the second time in my life, because my relationship with my baby's daddy, Garrett, had ended again. Fully submerged in postbreakup blues, I was unable to bounce back, and celebrate my independence; I was a shadow of my former self. I was too young to navigate safely away from what felt like heart-wrenching pain at the time. Intellectually, I wished I could take a ride in a time machine, going back to fix my relationship mistakes. Our time together seemed so short. Poof! Our days of being arm-in-arm were gone in a flash.

But my heart cried out, "How could I be reasonable? To me our love was all encompassing. You had become my world, my everything. How could you wreck, dismantle, destroy, and abandon our love?" Oh, how I wallowed in my own pain, unable to see that I had become my own worst enemy. The problem, of course, was simple—I nostalgically wandered in the archives of my past for far too long. I was definitely one of those people who needed a little motivation and reassurance to see beyond yesterday. It was difficult to break old patterns and enjoy my day-to-day life, keeping an eye out for any and all opportunities to emerge from despair.

My parents, in particular my mother, always pushed me to be a better version of myself. Their focus landed squarely on raising children to become the best they could be. Never giving in to my downtrodden attitude, they stressed that I should cope with my loss by becoming more educated and rising in the ranks of the workplace. Their idea of being better wasn't to become lost in ambition but to constantly work toward self-improvement. Instead of dealing with the grief from losing my relationship, I turned all my sorrow inward and began to punish myself through self-critical thoughts. Thankfully, advice my father passed on during this time certainly helped. He said, "The two most important days are today and tomorrow. Yesterday is gone, and there is nothing one can do to change that." Thank goodness, for that pearl of wisdom. I guess, father really does know what's best.

Looking back, I see I was blind to how truly fortunate I am to have such great parents. At that point in my life, I hadn't found a skill, interest, or talent that I excelled in or genuinely enjoyed. My parents were patient but wouldn't stand for laziness. Their house rules included my attending college full-time and securing a job in order to live rent-free. "Any job is better than no job," they kept repeating. I wasn't able to resolve my past, but I was encouraged to do whatever it took to get on with my life. Yes, more than a few things hadn't worked out, but I was urged not to give up, never give up. Finally, I picked myself up, got dressed, secured a waitress job, and enrolled as a part-time student at the local community college.

Waitressing didn't sound appealing to me, but I needed to stick with it, since I had a toddler at home. My son, Ryan, has been one of the greatest blessings in my life. Unknown to me at the time, my son's birth was a gift. So, I stopped crying about his father and our breakup, took more than a few deep breaths, and started my life over at twenty-three years old. It was so difficult trying to rebuild myself, piece by shattered piece, with no clue how to glue all the pieces back together.

Since I was sixteen, I had gained some experience waitressing. I knew it was one job that basically any woman could get and make quick cash to take home each and every shift. Thank goodness, I was hired at a local Perkins family restaurant in a neighboring town. Sure, I could always get stuck with bad tippers or a horrible shift, so taking this job was a crapshoot. It's a sad truth, but servers' federal minimum wage is a little over two dollars per hour, so their wages feel like tips, and their tips are their real wages. When you are young, it is almost impossible to take Confucius's advice: *"Choose a job you love, and you will never have to work a day in your life."*

I needed to work, because nothing in my life was working. Some memories stay with you your entire life. Funny, right? I will never forget that first day driving toward Perkins, nervous. It was critical that I made the right impression. "You never get a second chance to make a first impression," as the saying goes. New work environments always bring a certain level of stress, no matter how experienced you may be in that field. What really stood out on that ride toward work was that my dad informed me that I was only getting a one-way ride to work. I thought he was kidding. How could I secure a way home for myself? I just moved to Florida.

Within seconds, I knew my dad wasn't joking around. To this day, I think it was kind of a dick move to drop me off with no way home. Sure, my parents led busy lives and had other children and responsiblities, but why add extra stress to an already stressful situation? What parents don't juggle their time and responsiblities with their children? It was a fact of life that as their children, you had to figure out solutions to your own problems. There was always a shortage of transportation in our household. If we had a car, it wasn't working; if you had a driver's license, you had no wheels; and if somehow your car drove, then you couldn't really afford the gas.

How in hell did we endure those tough financial days? I vividly remember battling many momentary bouts of insanity asking why, why, and why life had to be so damn difficult. It was extremely nerve-racking, picturing how and who I would ask to drive me home. What had I gotten myself into? As I entered this famous pancake house, I looked around at my new coworkers. How would I hone in on which person looked friendly enough to ask for a favor? The thought of asking for help made me feel so uncomfortable. I began my training shift doing everything I could to possibly avoid asking that dreaded question.

I watched for clues, struggled to pay attention to those who seemed extra polite, sweet, even courteous. But the hospitality industry is fraught with selfishness, all the players out for themselves. This particular pool of employees didn't strike me as the type to go out of their way for a stranger, if you know what I mean. One of the head waitresses was training me that shift. I was to observe while adhering to her standards and pace, which was a full sprint, leaving little time for me to focus on the task of asking for help. Forget about impressing management; attaining better shifts is a far-off dream for a new employee.

The simplest task is taking the customer's order, but the wait time and delivery really fall upon the kitchen line. Becoming a server is definitely easy to learn but hard to master, since timing is everything. I had too many thoughts pervading, making training more challenging than it should have been. I was so frustrated with my dad. Why couldn't he have made things easier on me that day? My annoyance with him was gaining momentum in my thoughts. Then I spied someone in my peripheral vision who threw me off balance completely. Who caught my attention? Well, you wouldn't believe it unless you saw it yourself.

Imagine that you're shooting a basketball when a noise throws you off, making you miss what should have been an easy shot. My attention was grabbed by the sight of a woman walking through the dining room without any arms. Time stopped as this woman, wearing a sleeveless dress, limbless from the waist up, was escorting obviously uncomfortable customers to their seats. Was my mind playing tricks on me, or was this armless woman our restaurant's hostess? Yes, she was. As my mind asked this question, I noticed she was carrying menus between the nub of her one shoulder and a couple of limp fingers.

Honestly, it was like seeing an auto accident. I just couldn't help but rubberneck. Why do we turn our heads to see if there's anything gory? Human nature, I guess. Wide-eyed, I continued to watch as she managed seating arrangements. Truly, she was amazingly functional at her job, but I just couldn't stop staring. All my gawking was causing delays, and the head waitress frowned at my slower-than-expected pace. I know, I know, I was spending a lot of time standing there. Time is money, you know! And my trainer was concerned with her bottom line—making more money. I, on the other hand, was drawn to the humanity of this scene.

Truly, I felt my time wasn't wasted in watching her. She never rested as she greeted each customer. The weird thing about working in a restaurant is you notice patterns. The way people behave. When they enter a restaurant, most people are unable to wait patiently. Any delay is deemed intolerable. Restlessness sets in. By the time they reach the hostess stand, they are irritated and hungry, and they want the best the place has to offer. You know what I mean, right? They want the big booth by the window with the best view, and of course, they want it yesterday.

As well as that, they are totally unprepared to see is anything or anyone out of the ordinary. A hostess is the first employee to interact with each arriving guest. But as God is my witness, most—if not all—of the people who saw her coming toward them became scared. Unable to cope with her appearance, she caused a shock to their system, leaving them numb and unable to make eye contact. I have to admit that as I watched this scene unfold, I deep down really enjoyed each irate customer lose that high-and-mighty attitude. Again, call it human nature, but people can't always cope with an overwhelming physical disability. Some even see the physical condition as a threat.

Many times, new servers start in the section of the dining room without any booths, near the bathrooms. Of course, these are the least desirable places to sit for the customers, who believe they deserve the very best. But as our hostess started to lead each set of hungry customers toward one of these tables, they would relent—no objections, no complaints. Everyone would sit where she put them. This one disabled hostess had leveled the playing field, giving each server the chance to earn more tips, no matter what the assigned section.

Let's be candid. Most people, at least initially, can't see people beyond their physical disabilities. Honestly, every time our hostess dropped the menus from her tiny underdeveloped fingers, it looked like a ticker tape parade. Shit flew everywhere. The menus and inserts landed on the floor, chairs, and even on the table, leaving the customers scrambling, picking up the menus, and agreeing to sit anywhere. They wanted to end their misery and put an end to feeling so uncomfortable. It's this simple: people don't know how to behave around a person who is physically challenged.

I think there is an inate problem with the word 'disabilities' for it suggests an inability to perform an activity in the manner or within the range considered normal. Shouldn't the emphasis be on the person first without denying the reality of the disablity? These thoughts aside, I had to pull myself away from the human dynamics unfolding in front of me that day in order to address my needs. As my dinner break approached, I decided to take the opportunity to question a few of the staff. Who lived on the Cape? Once inside the tight, makeshift break room, I inquired about a lift home. A few disapproving looks were tossed my way, heads shaking no, and even a grunt or two. Then behind me, I heard the voice of a woman, kindly agreeing to drive me home. As

I turned to match the voice to a face, I was shocked to see the woman with no arms staring directly at me.

I tell this story not to make fun of anyone with a disability but to tell my story. Hell yes, I was upset and distressed by the thought of someone without any arms driving me home. Who were you in your early twenties? It is such a pivotal time in life; you're not emotionally mature but still striving to be a full-fledged adult. Remember, lots of young adults feel their life sucks. God forbid they get stood up for a date, or receive a speeding ticket, or find a large pimple on their face.

At that moment in time, all I could focus on is how much my life really sucked. I didn't think things could get any worse than being driven home by a complete stranger without arms. So while it wasn't a definite yes, I began to nod my head to her generous offer. Honestly, I am not going to defend myself or explain my behavior, but I was young, nervous, and a bit ignorant. For the remainder of my break, I ate quietly, watching the armless hostess eat with her feet. I was trying to imagine how she could even drive. Why was God or the universe forcing me to deal with a very unwanted situation? I didn't know if I could sidestep this set of circumstances I found myself in, so I made one last phone call to beg my parents for help.

My attempts for assistance were futile. Definitely, I was facing one of life's stumbling blocks. How I reacted, did in fact help define me. But that's not to say it wasn't a scary ride home. The experience was a stepping stone, towards being thankful, not only for the ride, but the opportunity to see things differently. After work, we met in the parking lot. As I peered into her car, I reviewed the odd accessories in pure fear. My stomach was in knots as she started the car. I kept my eyes straight ahead for the majority of the trip. But, occasionally, yes, I did glance over. I couldn't help it, curiosity got the best of me. What was it like? Well, I got kneed a few times, since she drove with her feet, but she did seem very comfortable behind the wheel.

Can you believe it? As she turned into my parents' driveway, she told me her house was just down the street. Of course, Mom and Dad found the whole story very entertaining. They went on to remind me that college doesn't have a monopoly on learning. I guess I have to agree with them. Now, I thank God for the opportunity to get to know this amazing woman. As time dragged on, I began to scrutinize my behavior and see things from her perspective. Our rides home became an opportunity to learn about her genetic birth defect and life as an artist. She was a foot painter, creating artwork with just her feet. Art allowed her to connect the spirit within life to her body and soul. Isn't it amazing how art gives people an escape from their afflictons?

Eventually I became closer to another, younger hostess, who told me the story of when the disabled hostess first was hired. Since she really uses her feet for everything, she actually hopped on one foot and carried and passed the menus with between her toes of the other foot. Honestly, I can't even imagine how this looked to incoming customers. One day, during lunch, a father dining with his wife and children lodged a complaint with the manager. He said he was all for the Americans with Disabilities Act, but in this specific case, something had to be done.

After being seated in a booth, his family had the misfortune to be handed menus by a foot. Not only did he find that not hygienic, but because she was wearing a dress, when she lifted her foot they saw her cooch. Talk about a negative experience at a restaurant!

I bet that manager got the shock of his life. The manager cowardly asked the younger hostess to get to the bottom of this situation, no pun intended.

"Are you wearing panties?" asked the younger hostess. "I can't," replied the armless hostess. "How would I put them on? I don't have any arms." How did she deal with going to the bathroom, or for that matter, her period? How many customers viewed her crotch before the solution was found?

It is so easy to overlook the universal human activities that people with disabilities struggle with daily. *"It has been said that life has treated me harshly; and sometimes I have complained in my heart, because many pleasures of human experience have been withheld from me...if much has been denied me, much, very much has been given me"* (Helen Keller).

My lesson was to treat any disabled person as I would treat a nondisabled person. I was selfish, thinking my life was tough, but after I got to know this inspirational human being, she actually disarmed me. When you look at her, you never think about the barriers she faced. She said that men didn't see disabled women in a sexual light. Finding love was difficult. Every man with whom she was intimate, she had to trust. Each time she had sex, it was a little like bondage. Without a doubt, this one woman has overcome adversity, by making a conscious effort to never place 'dis' in her ability.

Chapter 2:

WHAT'S BARBIE GOT TO DO WITH IT?

"I do have body-image issues, just like everyone else. I mean, I wish I had bigger boobs. And I hate my butt. I want an onion butt—you know, a butt that'll bring tears to your eyes."
—Leslie Bibb

I believe we are forced to meet people and experience certain situations in life that help us grow spiritually. Of course, I would have preferred my parents to drive me home from my first day working at Perkins, but the universe had different plans. Whether you know a person for an hour, a day, months, or years, they are in your life for the right amount of time, where you were meant to meet. There are no accidents; every person has something to teach us on a soul level. No matter how different people seem, even if they are incredibly irritating, they are in your life to teach you a lesson.

At first, my experience with the armless hostess seemed negative and very uncomfortable. But finally I realized meeting her gave me an opportunity to learn about compassion and empathy. I needed to be faced with the fact that there is always somebody who has it a lot worse than I do. Really, I believed I was justified in feeling sorry for myself, because I had been through a rough breakup. God must have known that this one woman would inspire me to stop my whining and just make my life work. Keeping an open mind and an open heart allowed me to start the healing process.

What I didn't know then was that I had to allow my inner child to heal. We all have an inner child, the part left behind in our subconscious that experienced childhood trauma. We may have grown up, but some of our dysfunctional issues need to be addressed. Once I cared for my inner child, there was a surprisingly quick healing process that took place. Inner-child issues cause extensive relationship issues, since we can try to get our needs met by others and not ourselves. To fully understand my relationship attachments, it is important that I share a bit of my childhood with you.

As a child, I adored Barbie. I spent the first decade of my life playing dolls and the next thirty years trying to look like one. No wonder I ended up in a Barbie world, where life was plastic. For a while, it seemed fantastic. I had the dream house, someone I believed was the perfect partner, and the life I'd imagined growing up. As a little girl, I was told that every fairy tale has a happy ending, yet I have struggled throughout my life to find that true bliss. Of course there were moments of happiness sprinkled here and there, but inside I was not truly fulfilled. I just know that there have to be others who also feel that they have not achieved their true potential.

During the past few years of my life, I have been reading self-help book after self-help book. After researching and soul-searching, I realized that I had been manifesting many unfulfilling things into my reality since childhood. Never would I have ever connected the dots from my play toys to the state of my actual existence. Even our play toys can have power, teach lessons, and guide our destiny.

I was born in the United States and moved to Ireland as a toddler. I ran freely through the fields, playing with my siblings and letting my imagination run wild. My surroundings were diverse, ranging from tranquil to magical. There was little value placed on money and having possessions. When I was seven years old, it was quite a shock to me, my sister, and my brothers to learn that we were leaving Ireland to return to America. But like most kids, we adapted quickly and viewed the move as a big adventure. My parents had a family meeting and told us that we had to give away all of our toys. Remember that, in the world of children, their toys are their treasures. Christmas after Christmas, birthdays, and major events are spent wishing for these items to add to their collection.

We were advised that only one toy would be allowed to travel with each of us to America. Yes! There were tears, screaming, and protests, because we were forced to give up our most prized possessions. I felt like the Godfather, willing all my property to my very best friends. My Daisy doll, which resembled a blond Bratz doll, was my chosen toy, my pride and joy. She would accompany me to our new home across the ocean. I don't remember much about the move, but I do remember the flights. We were to fly to New York and then on to Cleveland, Ohio. My father had left weeks before us, so he could find work and a home for his large family.

Once we boarded and settled into our assigned seats, I noticed Daisy was rather sleepy, so I decided to put her to rest in the magazine holder. I then took a nap. Before long we arrived in New York, and my mother shuffled her troop of six children off the plane. We rushed to meet our connecting flight to Cleveland. I was halfway to Cleveland when I realized Daisy was still sleeping in the magazine rack on our last plane. I was flooded with tears and sadness; I had lost my best friend and only toy. Devastated, I was a child without her toy, a girl without her doll, living in a new country, attending a new school. It was all too much. Losing her was one of my lessons: what happens when your heart breaks.

I had very little to play with for a while, but my parents did give us the gift of creativity. We really had to be more creative than smaller families, since we were on a limited budget. Within the first few weeks after we arrived in Cleveland, relatives donated toys, including Barbie dolls and GI Joes. But I had my heart set on getting a Ken doll that Christmas. Can you imagine my surprise to end up with a Donnie Osmond doll instead? Hell no! Donnie O. wasn't going to cut it, so I had Barbie reject him tirelessly until I finally I got a Ken doll. I believe that Daisy and Barbie were extensions of who I wanted to become—and who I actually did become on the surface—but that in reality left me hollow inside.

Oddly, my life has imitated the environment I dreamed up for my dolls. I was infatuated with the idea of one day growing up to look just like a doll. My very first real boyfriend in college was working toward becoming an officer in the marines. I think I met my GI Joe in him, right! My baby's daddy, who was the second man I fell in love with, holds a striking resemblance to a Ken doll. Okay, here's where it gets weird. My second husband looked just like Donnie Osmond. Honestly, he was tall with dark hair and really wanted my attention from the moment we first met. The fact is, I had manifested my playthings into my reality. I brought that which I intended for my life into actual existence in my physical world.

It is said, that our subconscious minds don't have a sense of humor or play any jokes upon us. For our subconscious doesn't know the difference between reality and imaginary thought. So, be careful what you continually think about because you too, can manifest both positive and negative thoughts into your lives. All of my hours of pretend play with Barbie— desiring to look like her and have boyfriends like her—paid off. Or did they? As a child, I aligned my thoughts and goals to bring me what I most desired. But there came a point in my adult life when I began to question my perfect Barbie life. Was it a dream or a delusion? Finally, it took a major heartache and a life-threatening illness to break free of my plastic, surface-only life.

Being a housewife, managing my household, and caring for my children had been all I ever dreamed of as a little girl. By my forties I was faced with a real reality check. Growing up, I never played any games that included Barbie's dream house facing foreclosure, Ken having addictions, or divorce. My inner child was trapped inside her very own self-inflicted Barbie bubble. It has been said that a girl playing with a doll anticipates the mother inside of her. But isn't it also true that lots of mothers are just children playing at parenthood. What's truer is the fact that both sexes equally can grow up to play at adulthood. We all grow taller and older, but there are times in our lives when we still feel like children inside, playing at being adults.

I am not going to say I didn't have many years of fun wearing pink-tastic clothes and dressing like up like a Barbie. I don't want to lie. I really did enjoy that part. As the years passed, I looked more and more like Barbie and I was becoming the perfect Stepford wife. It made perfect sense, since my views on beauty came directly from my time with my Barbie doll. Just think about it, I did become the blond Barbie doll of my dreams but that wasn't enough to create inner happiness. Still, it took years to discover who I am, from the inside out.

But by my thirties, I was becoming plastic, really plastic. It's easy to get absorbed in making money, owning expensive automobiles. Another, bigger problem became the men whom I had attracted into my life. Truly, each husband was fake, plastic, a taker, a user, even a wannabe elitist. My second husband was definitely the kind of man who wanted a Barbie doll on his arm. He went out of his way to sculpt every facet of his image. You know, wining and dining me at expensive restaurants yet rarely being seen in public doing anything that affected his image negatively. But that's not what was going on in private; Donnie O.'s mask had to drop at some point.

Really, it's not what's wrong with Barbie, but what was innately wrong with me as a person. Let's face it, for heaven's sake, Barbie is just a doll. I was the one holding onto the illusion that I had to be perfect. Agreed, the delusion started at a young age, but how many girls did (and will) grow up with Barbie as their image of beauty and perfection? For many of us, the truth is hidden behind illusions that society and our environment create around who we "should" be. After all, who doesn't want to morph into a beautiful, sexy icon? That's what we believe men are attracted to, right?

You, see, your forties can be your best friend. Finally, you realize that you've spent decades exercising, dieting, and perfecting your exterior for someone else's pleasure. If you are anything like me, you've been trapped in a vicious cycle of not feeling good enough. So I take you on a journey through two marriages with men who believed they were sex gods.

And Barbie, what's she got to do with it? Well, I gotta give it up to her. She provided me with some of my greatest lessons in life. As Ellen DeGeneres said, *"Beauty is all about being comfortable in your own skin. It's about knowing and accepting who you are."*

For me, it took some time to learn that outer beauty pleases others while inner beauty pleases you. So often in my life I had a tendency to take things at face value. Unsure of myself, I believed what others told me without question or thought of ulterior motives or hidden meanings. Those who stood to benefit from slight deceptions and hidden truths were somehow drawn to me.

The more eye-catching I became, the more I resembled a thing, like a shiny new car. Believe me; it took a lot of courage to dive below the surface of my plastic life. In facing those men I loved, whom I called my best friends, I had to balance their actions with their words. It didn't matter what they looked like. Jess C. Scott said, *"What's the whole point of being pretty on the outside when you're so ugly on the inside?"*

Throughout my journey I had to learn to face my deepest, darkest secrets. Emotional insecurities were holding me back, leaving me feeling vulnerable and inferior. To find my confidence again, I would need to remove all doubt about who I really was. At my core I had feelings of being unloved and unworthy, and I constantly blamed myself for everything. It came as no surprise to learn that trying to perfect myself came from the desire to please others and prove to myself I was worthy.

The sum of my emotional traumas left me with shattered self-esteem and a feeling of self-hate. Feeling unwanted and rejected left a huge hole in both my heart and soul. My depression was intense at times, stemming from all of my anxiety about losing my sense of self that, sadly, was dependent on another. I let my self-reliance and self-confidence lie in the hands of another human being. And until I chose to build a solid foundation of sustainable self-love and self- respect, I would never know the roots of my own soul.

I have to admit, there was a time where I was so fake, Barbie would have been jealous. Hell, if a man wants perfection, then he should head to the toy store and purchase his own Barbie doll! And how is it that boys play with toys growing up too, but you don't hear them spending the rest of their lives feeling inadequate about their lack of super-powers. Ironically, men feel more inadequate about the toys girls play with as adults. They'd rather compete with a dick-less Ken doll than a 10-inch cock that vibrates. Hey, I'm just sayin'.

Still, I want to tell my story, in the hope that I also tell other women's stories, and while I find my voice, I hope to aid others in finding their voice as well. I strongly recommend you learn to speak your truth. It will free you like nothing else you have ever experienced. Spiritual healing became the key to unlocking my true self and finally helping me find real fulfillment in my life. Maybe I'm not a New Age guru, but I am a big believer in the mind-body-spirit movement. All of my life lessons came from overcoming life's hurts. But once I looked within myself, I discovered who God really wanted me to be.

I can't stress how important it was that I addressed the wounded little girl inside of me whose hopes and dreams for the perfect marriage and family had been destroyed forever. My first book, *Barbie: A Parody*, was done as a comedic takedown on the Barbie doll iconic image, in order to highlight the contradictions and hypocrisies of relationship issues. The fact remains that over one billion women have played with Barbie at some point in their lives. But relationship dissolution never existed anywhere in Barbie fantasyland. My inner child found a brief respite from the stress and tension of her relationship failures. I promise you—there really is hope. You too can heal the wounded child inside of you and move on to fully enjoy your life.

Chapter 3:

PREGNANT AND PRAYING

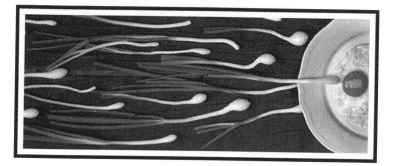

(Unknown Photographer)

"Does anyone ask their parents how they are conceived?"
—Boris Becker

To be honest, my most difficult life lessons came from my failed relationships. Growing up a wannabe Barbie doll, I tended to attract men who reflected the things that I believed about myself, love, and relationships. Some of my life lessons came easily, like meeting the awe-inspiring hostess, but there were times I failed to learn my lessons. Now I realize that both of my marriages were opportunities to do the right thing by myself. Had I built my boundaries and said no after my first divorce, I wouldn't have been drawn into a second marriage to make a different choice.

It took an inordinate amount of time to believe that my failed marriages served to teach me more about myself. After my first divorce, I continued to do the same thing, but I expected a different result, which we all know is relationship insanity. Like a lot of you, I had to stop, take time, and recognize my relationship patterns if I was ever going to evolve and really change. Trust me; I have had my fill of drama and being chased, only to end up getting deeply hurt and emotionally scarred. I was sheltered as a teen, with a strict curfew, which of course backfired later, causing me to rebel in college.

College really is the best time of your life. Who doesn't love partying from dawn to dusk and dusk to dawn? There were no rules. Total freedom. I thoroughly enjoyed the alcohol and partying lifestyle. I started college as a virgin, but by the end of the first semester that had all changed. Forget about my studies, I was experiencing real life for the first time in my life. After pledging to be a little sister at my older brother Kieran's fraternity house, I was introduced to Derrick, an upperclassman. At first we didn't like each other, but then we shared one long weekend, and sparks flew.

Our relationship lasted one volatile year. Derrick won me over by showering me with compliments, expensive gifts, and his time. He was the first man I was ever intimately involved with, and we enjoyed a variety of sexual and erotic acts. As time progressed, a sexual downward spiral occurred as Derrick pushed my boundaries. Often he would manipulate me into what he wanted during sex, even when I was reluctant to go with Derrick's desires. Sure, there were times he was playful, even loving; nevertheless, I knew I had to leave this passionate but destructive relationship.

Now I realize that Derrick was my manifestation of my brother's GI Joe doll, my first doll's boyfriend. Of course, I met Derrick in college, but every summer he would return to training in order to become an officer in the marines. For a while, GI Joe was the only boy doll I could get my little hands on. Ironically, he always arrived at Barbie's dream house in his jeep, without any pants on. Derrick was definitely a man of action, but he was also a man who didn't know how to love me. I knew if I didn't eventually leave him, I would have an emotional breakdown, so I called off our relationship.

Derrick was incredibly angry. He felt deserted and devastated, yet he still found reasons to show up at my home, my sorority. I just couldn't deal with Derrick's need not to share me with anyone. There was no way I was going let our relationship take center stage. I just wanted my independence. Just as I was breaking things off with Derrick, Garrett arrived on the scene. He was better-looking than Derrick, more all-American in his looks—tall, blond, and blue-eyed, and he was a former high-school jock. I have to admit it; my little girl's dreams had just come true. I was standing in front of a real-life Ken doll.

On what seemed like an ordinary Saturday night, the doorbell rang, and there he was, a Phi Sigma Kappa, surrounded by his frat brothers. This group of guys had showed up in order to serenade the Alpha Zi Deltas. Their mission was to sell tickets for a fund-raiser, but really they wanted to drown coeds in booze while living out their naughty fantasies. A few of us, including me, attended their charity event, which turned into something loosely like a Chippendale's revue. Our waiters for the evening were shirtless, with little white bow ties around their necks. Their jiggly beer bellies hung over the dress pants as they flirted tirelessly with us.

God forgive me, but truly, we were forced to watch some of the ugliest male strippers execute terrible dance moves that night. Between the crotch thrusting, body butter, and free alcohol, I puked for most of the ride home. Their striptease show was hardly captivating, but it made for great laughs. As the winner of the evening's door prize, I was awarded a date with any of the brothers at the event. Of course, I chose my Ken doll—Garrett,

He was someone I thought my parents would love for their daughter to date, not to mention I thought he was really hot!

I agreed to a first date, not entirely sure that I would go on a second. I mean really, most of his friends or frat brothers were just Neanderthal douche bags. Surprisingly, Garrett came off as quite a gentleman. I just loved the simplest gestures, like when he opened his car door for me. He also earned major brownie points when he took off his jacket and draped it over my shoulders as it became colder outside. We talked all night, in between cuddling and making out, of course. Somehow, he won me over with his schoolboy charm, although as I look back, our sex was hard to quantify.

How do you measure great sex when you have only been with one other partner? With Derrick, the sex was reckless, untamed, and mainly pleasure seeking, but there was no depth or intimacy.

What I didn't bargain for at that point in my life was being faced with an unplanned pregnancy. I was flabbergasted when I discovered my predicament. What did I expect? I mean really, I was so stupid to trust

Garrett's favorite mode of birth control—withdrawal. So what if he hated condoms? I needed to be more responsible for my body. At least I can find humor in finding out that the slang word today for sex without a condom is "raw."

I was incredibly naïve about protecting my fertility. There were no "open and frank" discussions about sex in the Burke household when I was growing up. The mere mention of the word would make my Irish Catholic parents extremely uncomfortable. Really, I can't put the blame on my parents for my lack of judgment; I ultimately was to blame for my own decisions, or lack thereof. I owe my life to my parents, and I love them, but it would have been nice to have been better prepared for the consequences of unprotected sex.

Finally, I broke down and took the cowardly way out. I told them I was pregnant over the phone. In shock, my mother lost her grip on the pan. Splat went the baked fish for dinner. My news had caused a chain reaction. The fish landed butter-side down on the kitchen floor. I remember wondering if she was going to apply the five-second rule, dust it off, and serve it to my siblings.

I was worried about my new relationship with Garrett. It was fragile, still in the early stages. Garrett opened up, telling me he had been through a pregnancy scare with his high-school sweetheart. They agreed to an abortion and continued with their college plans. That said…it wasn't long till Garrett was begging me to get a quick abortion. And soon, everyone was adding their two cents; even one of my sorority sisters advised me to terminate my pregnancy. I disregarded her advice, since she had had multiple abortions. Was it all right to use abortion as birth control? I didn't think so.

Pressure was building at home; my parents, Michael and Christina, really wanted me to keep their first grandchild. Coming from Ireland, they were devoted Catholics. But secretly, I always wondered whether they were a bit careless to have had so many children. It remains a mystery how my parents handled it. Even the Brady Bunch had Alice. Call it synchronicity, but during this difficult decision process, God sent me an angel—my aunt Martha. She pointed me toward Planned Parenthood, so I could choose life or death. I must admit it was difficult to enter the building for my appointment after laying eyes on the words BABY KILLERS splashed across the front doors.

As the counselor spoke of my need to have a saline abortion, I impulsively moved my hands protectively cover my swollen belly. I had my answer in that moment. There was no way in hell anyone was killing my baby with a lethal injection of concentrated salt water. Wow! I didn't know what maternal instincts felt like until that very day. I learned early in my pregnancy. Reluctant to put my child up for adoption, I committed to having my child. Would I judge someone who has had an abortion? I try not to; it really is a woman's choice. I believe God is the ultimate judge, not man.

Deciding to keep my child was a lesson in reconciling my praxis with my heart—looking in the mirror and understanding that I wouldn't have any regrets whatsoever with my decision. Wholeheartedly, I committed to becoming the very best mother I could be. God only knows how I persevered, deep in the trenches of an unexpected pregnancy. Garrett abandoned me and his child. As he harshly told me we were done, my eyes filled with tears. His parents felt I was trapping him by having our child. I attempted suicide that very night, believing life wasn't worth living if I had to go through this journey alone.

I grabbed one of Garrett's razors, and I started to cut my wrists in a horizontal direction. Since there is a lot of tendon and gristle, I was unable to get the job done. The emotional pain was excruciating. Why had I allowed him to hurt me? I might as well have given him the razor because his rejection cut me to the core. God, I felt like a complete failure, I couldn't even kill myself correctly. How was I going to be someone's mother? My suicidal attempt pushed Garrett further away. It was extremely depressing going to Lamaze classes and doctor's appointments alone. I knew nothing about childbirth. Days, weeks, and months passed. Of course, my body and baby grew as I struggled silently with depression. Were the odds against me raising a healthy, happy child? The experience of pregnancy was mainly an unpleasant and uncomfortable experience, yet I had moments of joy. One of those moments was the discovery I was to have a little boy.

My baby appeared on the ultrasound screen looking more like a little peanut. Then the nurse pointed out his "itty-bitty, teeny-weeny." I was thrilled my firstborn was a boy; I had an older brother and wanted that for my family. Only a few friends kept in contact with me. And there were a few more so-called friends who just called to gossip about Garrett and his philandering. These calls kept me spiraling emotionally downward. Each juicy tidbit hurt me deeply. I always pretended the news didn't hurt, but it did, it really did. As the birth of my child approached, I began suffering from tokophobia—fear of childbirth.

I also didn't do so well with wearing the ugly nursing bras and pads. I admit that I was grossed out by the colostrum, the early breast milk that began to leak. By my ninth month I was fully in the throes of loathing my body. Then a stranger hit on me while I was getting gas. Of course, I refused his advances telling him I was pregnant. But he insisted that I was lying and became angry. Part of me was flattered, no one had flirted with me in months, and the other part of me was insulted. Who did this loser think he was, insisting I show him my belly?

The inevitable end to any pregnancy is birth, no matter how long and lonely. I still wished I didn't have to go through childbirth. Why couldn't the doctor just knock me out so I'd feel nothing, and then I could wake up and be handed a beautiful little baby? Just like in some of the old TV shows I used to watch. I had actually reached the end of my emotional rope. I dropped to my knees in prayer. "Lord, I can't go on, my load is too heavy. Please let me raise my child until he reaches the age of twenty-one. Then you can take my life!" Yes, I was bargaining with the Lord, exchanging my life for my son's welfare, and somehow I felt better, safer.

No, I wasn't a fan of natural childbirth; I wanted any and all drugs that were being offered. My birth cocktail included an epidural and spinal block, thank God. I'm sure if Eve had had a choice she would have jumped at pain meds when she gave birth. As you know, I have admitted to doing all I can to avoid pain wherever and whenever possible. Lucky for me, labor lasted only six hours. Then my doctor placed my baby boy on my belly. I will never forget how warm he felt, and when we locked eyes, it was as if we had always known each other. Words can't explain how much unconditional love I felt toward him.

Ryan Michael Burke was born on December 16, 1989. He was true perfection. Thank goodness, my mother, a nurse, was there with me to usher this little person into the world. It took days before Garrett even showed up at the hospital. He didn't want to sign Ryan's birth certificate. Can you believe he had the nerve to say he wasn't sure he was even the baby's father? And when he did arrive, all I heard was his complaints about pain from a minor skiing accident that month. Was he joking? I wanted to throw back my blankets to reveal the extensive damage to my vagina. It must have looked like the site where two trains had collided.

Finally, I got to take my child home. We wrapped him in several blankets because of the frigid weather. Back then, I wasn't required to have a car seat, so I held him the entire forty-minute ride home. Once home, I discovered I had held him upside down on my shoulder for the entire ride. What kind of mother was I? I felt like an idiot. The blood had rushed to his head and caused his little face to turn bright red. Yet I forged on, and within a month of his birth, I returned to Kent State University to resume my education. Secretly, I hoped to get back with Ryan's father and work on becoming a family. I was living alone with my child in a special dorm for unwed mothers and families.

It didn't take long for Garrett to show up, eat my food, and play with my emotions. I was shocked to find out at my postpartum checkup that he had given me chlamydia as a push present. What a dick! Luckily, simple medication cured the STD, but my broken heart was not as easy to treat. Foolishly, I forgave Garrett. He swore his devotion to both the baby and me. How could I refuse him? Jesus preached forgiveness. Caring for a newborn was a full-time job. And on top of that, I was attending college full time and working part time as a bartender. Garrett didn't pay support or care for his son. He was so selfish while I was so, so stupid.

As that spring semester came to an end, my car broke down, and my employer went out of business. It was impossible to be independent, so I decided to move back with my parents. But they had moved to Florida. One accomplishment was that I had earned straight As.

Disappointed that Garrett had not invited Ryan or me to his graduation, I called off our relationship. He made me feel as if we were his dirty little secrets. What a slap in the face. It was the wake-up call that I needed to get on with my life. I moved to Florida while Garrett remained in Ohio, to become a manager at Bob Evans.

I only stayed with my parents a short time, since Garrett wanted Ryan and me back in his life. We moved to Columbus, and I started attending Ohio State University while working part time at a day care. Garrett proposed romantically on an old wooden Ohio bridge, and I happily said yes! Finally, our struggles were over. Or were they?

As the wedding plans began, I felt Garrett becoming more distant. With only a few months till our big day, Garrett insisted we visit his parents' home. Imagine my surprise when he told me he felt pressured to marry me and wasn't ready to be a husband or father. What a selfish asshole, bringing me to his parents' house, when he could have broken off the engagement at our apartment.

I was mortified in front of his family. While I was crying, Garrett's mother offered to keep Ryan, but I knew better than leave my child. We had never been separated. He was my whole world. Frantically, I called my brother Kieran; thank goodness he drove two hours that night to rescue us. He was in law school, the last member of my immediate family to live in the area. This break up hit me hard. I felt empty and restless. I waited for Garrett to call. There had to be a better explanation. I lost interest in my appearance, living in an old pink robe and not showering for days.

Each day seemed to drag as I continued to cry and wail. How did I let this happen again? What an idiot! Raw emotions bled out as my brother looked on, bewildered. I was sinking into a deep depression. As much as my brother wanted to help, he couldn't. But that didn't stop him from trying. Kieran insisted on getting movies and a pizza to cheer me up. At the same time, my parents were making flight arrangements for us to return to Florida, where I would soon meet a woman who would snap me out of my depression. Yes sir, God works in mysterious ways.

No sooner did Kieran return with the pizza than the phone rang. Instinctively, I knew it was Garrett. I disappeared into the bedroom to take the personal call.

We spoke for what felt like forever, yet accomplished nothing. There was no real explanation for his actions, no apologies, just a hint of the thread of guilt he felt. Kieran began yelling at me to get off the phone and come enjoy the movie he rented. When I finally hung up the phone, I sat down on the couch next to Ryan. Sobbing, I reached for my cup of orange soda. As I took a gulp of soda, I felt something stick to the roof of my mouth. I gagged. "Gawk, gawk, gawk."

Kieran spit out his soda, laughing hysterically. I began to rush toward the bathroom, starting to puke. Confused, I returned to ask Kieran what the hell had just happened. Tears flowed down his face; he wasn't able to control his laughter. My brother told me the story. I couldn't believe my ears. While I was taking the call from Garrett, he had picked a thin, slippery booger from his nose and fired it across the room. It had miraculously landed on the interior of my beverage. It was a million-to-one shot. His mucus rolled down the side of the cup and was camouflaged in the orange soda.

Laughing still, Kieran apologized. Honestly, he meant to replace my beverage, but he became so enthralled in the film that he forgot all about picking his nose. Oh my God! *Disgusting*! Could my life get any worse? Really, how many people do you know who have eaten someone else's booger? I was horrified. But luckily, today I can see the humor in the midst of my despair. I have long since forgiven Kieran, but I never did find out if eating boogers has any health benefits. Again a lesson: Laugh through the tears. Life can get worse. It's all about perspective, and trust me, when you change your perspective, you can change your whole world.

Chapter 4:

WHEN LIGHTNING STRIKES

"When all else fails, there's always delusion."
Conan O'Brien

As you know, this is when I returned yet again to Florida for family support. Although wouldn't you know it, just when I became the center of my world, Garrett wanted me back. I must have had a brain fart, forgetting that our last breakup was brutal and all. I mean, wake-up Fiona, did you forget about our turbulent past and the cruel way he dumped you? Yet, somehow our flame rekindled, and I accepted his second marriage proposal. I know, I know. I was a fool in love. With the guidance of my parents, we enrolled in Pre-Cana class, so we could have a full-blown Catholic service. Father Fagan, a good friend of my father, agreed to marry us. Our hearts felt so big and bright as we started planning a big June wedding.

Kudos to me, cause looking back; I must have been one of the first to start that destination wedding trend. Up until that point in time, most of my extended European family had never experienced Florida's sandy beaches, amazing scenery, and gorgeous warm weather. But instead of focusing on all those positives, our big day was filled with a few too many negatives. Really, our wedding was more like a series of unfortunate events. First, I hadn't yet noticed that South Florida hosts only two seasons: rainy and dry. So naïvely, I took the sunshine for granted. Thus of course, it rained on our wedding day. But I wasn't entirely sure if that meant good or bad luck. Later I read that raindrops represent the many tears a bride with shed during her married life. I believe it.

Another odd moment was as I arrived at the church. My grandma Beatty, my mother's mother, whispered in my ear that I didn't have to go through with this marriage. Did she know something I didn't? Again, I brushed off yet another warning sign of things to come. As I followed my little son, our ring bearer, down the aisle on my father's arm, I focused solely on Garrett, who looked like a frozen statue. I knew it—he was paralyzed by fear. As he took my hand, his sweat dripped from his forehead onto my arm. It was hard not to notice that his heart was pounding—so much so, it looked like it might explode out of his chest.

Maybe I should have listened to Grandma Beatty's warning. I tried to listen to Father Fagan. He was joyful in his tone as he said, "Bless O, Lord, this ring to be a sign of the vows by which this man, with all that he is and all that he has, will honor his wife, in the name of the father, and of the son, and of the holy spirit." But then all of a sudden thunder, accompanied a lightning bolt, hit the glass canopy in the center of the church's cathedral ceiling. Are you kidding me? Still, I didn't see this as my third warning sent directly from heaven. Talk about putting blinders on!

Father Fagan laughed and lightened the moment by saying, "Thank God, lightning never strikes the same place twice," and he resumed the mass. Okay, I wanted to ignore these omens; we did live in the lightning capital of the world. Maybe I should have hoped for the best and planned for the worst. But I am a hopeless romantic, believing that one's wedding day was as good as it gets. So after church, we headed for cocktail hour and photographs at my parents' home. There we stood in my father's flower garden in the front yard, taking photo after photo.

As Ryan put up with many a cheek pinch from adults admiring how cute he was, I started to feel dizzy. Straining to smile, I began to overheat. Nauseated, I ran inside toward my mother's room. But she wouldn't help, preoccupied with taking stitches out of my younger brother Pat's ass. He had had a basketball accident earlier that month. So I ran directly into the guest room, tearing off my wedding dress, only to see hundreds of red ants swarming the lining of the dress. I had been bitten too many times to count and was having a full-blown allergic reaction to the bites.

Can you believe it; I had unknowingly stood right on top of an ant nest while posing for photographs. Somehow, my father had forgotten to throw down pest control that week. So, I was rushed to the nearest emergency room, still wearing my bridal veil, to receive a shot of steroids to bring down the massive swelling. My nose had blown up to twice its normal size. I promise you it was not a pretty sight. The ER doctor advised me to stay away from alcohol that night, so I couldn't even enjoy a single glass of champagne that day. Hours later, when I finally arrived at the reception hall, our guests greeted me with a standing ovation. To complete this nightmare, my new husband, Garrett, got completely wasted and woke up with a major hangover.

I can't count how many times I'd played out my wedding day with Barbie and Ken, but trust me, not one time did any of these events come into my mind. Sometimes the reality of a situation really does bite! But still, we had a lot of family in town, so we delayed our honeymoon a few days in order to enjoy their company. Luckily, one of my most prized memories came during this delay. The entire family gathered at a local Irish pub to rehash the wedding down to the last detail. As the men played darts, I found a comfy seat between my grandmothers. Who knew I was going to have one of the best conversations about sex with them that evening?

Each was full of vim and vigor, incredibly lively. They taught me that age really isn't anything more than a number. Funny thing is, I thought I was going to teach them a thing or two about sex—you know, maybe shock them a little bit. But as we drank our wine, I soon realized that these women were too smart for my BS. At first, I hit them with a little game of "Do you know what a _____ is?" Their eyes lit up. My questions began to pique their interests. It wasn't often anyone discussed sex with either of them. God, blame it on the booze, but I asked if they knew what a "pearl necklace" was.

They giggled as they agreed it must be fine jewelry. No, no, no, I said, it's when a man ejaculates all over a woman's neck after thrusting his penis between her breasts. They laughed and said in their Irish accents, "Oh come on, now, no woman would let a man do that to her." I was the one in shock that what I said hadn't gotten a bigger reaction. So I proceeded to ask if they knew what a jelly donut was, and not the Dunkin Donuts type. I told them I was recently informed that a jelly donut describes the state of a man's face after performing oral on a woman while she's on her period. Shocked, they spit out their drinks, laughing and repulsed at the same time. It was at this point my father walked by and overheard what I had just said to his mother.

I do believe I traumatized my father more than my grandmothers. It was difficult for them to comprehend that any man would be into menstrual sex. There my dad stood, with his mouth wide open; he looked as if he'd seen a ghost. He asked me to stop the conversation, stop it right now. But his mother, laughing like a schoolgirl, told him "Ah, go away with ya...we're having fun!" Interestingly enough, each grandma wanted to know what the other's sex life entailed; I was their personal go-between. They never divulged any details but really enjoyed the moment, maybe even more than I did.

Sadly, but not without warning signs, within the first few months Garrett and I were barely coexisting. We argued over everything, from bills to partying. He wanted us to split every bill, and whoever made more should reap the rewards on the weekends. I found it totally unfair, not only because I made less, but because he chose to spend his time drinking outside of our home. He had major commitment issues. And on top of that he started using cocaine, without my knowledge. Now, there was one time I noticed white powder in his room in college, but he swore he wasn't into drugs. Boy, oh boy, was I gullible.

On the surface, Garrett appeared to be a good-looking family man, but secretly he lived a lifestyle of excessive drinking mixed with a cocaine addiction. He was a high-functioning addict, able to get up for work no matter what happened the previous night. Lucky for us, an acquaintance, Stephanie, stepped up to offer us some marital counseling. She worked as a case manager for the Florida Department of Children and Family Services and knew a thing or two about family therapy. We were introduced to her by my sister Deirdre, who rented a room from her that she shared with her boyfriend, Chase.

Really, I was grateful for the help, and she did teach me a thing or two about how not to fight with your partner. Don't bring in old arguments, stuff like that. I thought it was odd that we were having so many issues— we weren't even married for six whole months. Things came to a head (pun intended, you'll see) within a month and a half of starting therapy. I wanted to give our son, Ryan, a special birthday, so I cooked a meal and baked a cake. Trust me, I am no Emeril Lagasse or Betty Crocker, but I put in some effort. To my dismay, when Garrett arrived home for work, he had other plans. He wanted to head out to a party. I had hoped he changed his mind.

But I became hysterical when I discovered he had slipped out through the back sliders. I can't tell you how hurt I was for Ryan—and for myself. As I wept, I managed to make a call to my mother, who said, "If you can't beat them, join them." She is an astute woman, always knowing just what to say. So first, Ryan and I celebrated his big day with mama's home cooking. Then after presents were opened, I decided to dress up and drop our son off at my parents' house. As I headed toward that party I remember feeling uneasy. Just as I arrived, I looked in the front window, witnessing Garrett in all his glory. He was, of course, hammered. How I wished he could have had that much fun with Ryan and me, but I brushed off the thought and went inside.

Everyone was passing around a bottle of Goldschlager cinnamon schnapps. Round after round, people threw back shots. The hostess of the event was none other than our counselor, Stephanie. I was so overwhelmed by the swarms of assholes, both drunk and high, that I caved in. I decided to call it a night. There was no way I was going to catch a buzz and chill out. No sooner had I returned home after picking up Ryan, than I found Deirdre and Chase on my doorstep, urging me to return to the party for Garrett. Hyper, they insisted something didn't feel right; they had seen Stephanie licking Garrett's fingers. Gross! But seriously, my sister said that was a sexual act, and I should be worried.

It might sound mean, but I couldn't see Garrett being attracted to Stephanie, not because she was our therapist, but because she was overweight. I'm gonna guess she was about a deuce, deuce and a half, maybe more. But since Deirdre pleaded with such intensity, I decided to return to the scene of the finger-sucking crime. Honestly, I had to play a mind game with myself. How I would feel if Stephanie was one of the most beautiful women, would I then be jealous? Hell, yeah, I would, so I proceeded forward. The first thing I noticed when I pulled up in front of her lawn was that the blinds were closed. What intoxicated people think of closing the blinds? So I didn't knock; I just threw open the front door. And to my surprise, Stephanie was giving my newly married husband a blow job.

There she was in all her glory, with my spouse's penis in her mouth, turning toward me to say, "Hellllooo!" Of course, Garrett was sitting on the couch, his head thrown back and his eyes rolling around in his head. He was barely conscious, yet he managed to whimper and moan in ecstasy. What a pig! My eyes filled with tears as I awkwardly backed out the door, traumatized, yet speechless.

On my way home, I heard a siren and saw glowing red lights in my rearview mirror. I had unknowingly run a stop sign and was being pulled over. As the female officer asked for my license and registration, I blurted out, "Newlywed…husband...b—blow—blow job…with our counselor!"

She could see I was emotionally distressed and decided not to give me a ticket. Truly, I was blessed, since she took pity on me and offered to give me a police escort home. You can image Deirdre's and Chase's faces when they saw me return home behind a cop car. They were beyond puzzled. Funny thing about certain memories, you don't forget them, instead recalling each and every vivid detail. Yes, even my little blow job story had a lesson—to not judge a book by its cover, because backstabbing comes in all shapes and sizes!

Chapter 5:

AGREED, LIFE IS LIKE A BOX OF CHOCOLATES

"An onion can make people cry, but there's never been a vegetable that can make people laugh."
—Will Rogers

"It ain't over until the fat lady sings," they say, but sadly, my marriage wasn't over when the fat lady gave fellatio either. My first marriage continued, because I refused to learn my lessons on betrayal. To love is to allow another to deliberate be disloyal. This can only happen if you love. Again, it took time for me to realize that there are benefits in life's negative, painful moments. I know the world is messy and imperfect. It has and always will be imperfect. And I am certainly not going to be about to change that fact. My job is to work as hard as I can on tidying up my own life.

I'm just gonna have to agree with Forrest Gump's mama. She's the one who said, "Life is like a box of chocolates. You never know what you're gonna get." Now I see that marriage is similar to a large, beautifully wrapped box of chocolates. As time passed, our relationship included a variety of flavors that I never asked for or wanted. Unfortunately, there was no returning this half-eaten, stomach-turning gift. What I didn't bargain for was a marriage to an addict, who conveniently always claimed amnesia in the morning to avoid taking responsibility for his terrible actions.

Sure the bible says *"Love is patient; love is kind; love is not envious or boastful or arrogant or rude. It does not insist on its own way; it is not irritable or resentful; it does not rejoice in wrongdoing but rejoices in the truth. It bears all things, believes all things, hopes all things, and endures all things" (1 Corinthians 13:4–7).* Although if I am going to remain honest, I have to say I don't think I have ever experienced that kind of love. Come to think of it, what the hell is love anyway? All I know, is love shouldn't hurt and if it does then it's something else like attachment, fear, or addiction.

Seriously, it took too long to discover that love is not what the moves and hit songs say it is. What I do know is that love is not only blind, it's also deaf, dumb, and, let's face it, stupid. Over and over, I compromised my own values for the sake of creating harmony within our family. Really and truly, I shouldn't have compromised myself, I was all I had and I was putting myself and our child in danger.

Sadly, I believed our marriage was definitely a big box of assorted chocolates, seemingly worthy of tasting. But really each piece of candy was completely inedible; yet I kept digging in, eating piece after nasty piece. It wasn't just the first year of marriage that was rocky, it was every year after that, too. For four long and painful years I endured his temper, affairs, even physical abuse. At first it started with being awakened in the middle of the night with icy hands around my neck, choking the life out of me. It progressed to a knife at my throat in front of our young son, all the way up to the last incident, when he came up behind me to punch me in the back of my head. Honestly, I had heard that alcohol brings out your true feelings, but I didn't want to face the truth: my husband secretly hated and resented me.

You would think after I ate a few of those disgusting pieces of chocolate I would have learned. Maybe packed up and left, right? Nope. I didn't walk away, which probably leaves you asking "why in the hell not?" You see, I wanted the violence to stop, not the relationship to end. And yet there was this part of me that believed the abuse must have somehow been my fault. If I could have been a better wife...this was my logic to allow Garrett to get away with abuse—verbal, emotional, and physical. Forget about yucky chocolates. It didn't take too long before I started eating shit sandwiches. And boy oh boy, I've eaten enough poop sandwiches for a lifetime. Like the time, I was forced to clean up after my husband's bedwetting—on and off the bed—due to his excessive drinking. Believe me; I gagged more than a little knowing no part of our home was unscathed.

All of the chaos Garrett created left me thinking about fixing him before myself. Since I couldn't deal with my marriage problems, I controlled my weight. Call it guilt, shame, or a mixture of the two, but I had acquired an uncontrollable urge to purge. I rarely binged but often purged, with my weight sometimes dropping to unhealthy levels. There are all sorts of addictions that can and do destroy families, careers, and even lives. Let's face it, all addictions—whether alcohol, drugs, or bulimia—shield you from intolerable pain. But I'll have to admit, that still to this day, my number one addiction has to be that of being a love addict; it has and always will be a hard habit to kick.

Obviously, with Barbie and Ken as my idols, I found romantic love something to aspire to. Romantic love became my drug of choice. Sadly, when I fell in love, I became powerless, as if I were under a spell. I lost my ability to make wise choices for me and my child. Love was the most important thing in my world. My relationship with Garrett proved love is not a fairy tale. No matter how much work, perseverance, and patience I put forth, I could not save our marriage. It was inevitably doomed. It would have needed the two of us to make our relationship work, not one.

Much of the time, our marriage felt like we were swimming upstream, getting nowhere. I was barely treading water, and then Garrett insisted we have another child. He longed for a parenting mulligan, since he felt that he had messed up raising Ryan. I didn't understand his logic: having another when his firstborn was here, alive, needing, and wanting his father's attention. I finally agreed

One ominous night during my third trimester I woke up surrounded by darkness to discover that Garrett had never arrived home. That endless night I lay awake, shedding tears, seeking an answer to why he never came home. I closed my eyes and prayed that he would come walking through our front door. After a while I relinquished my hopes that soon he'd be slipping into bed next to me. Determined, I woke up our kindergartner, strapped him in his car booster seat, and drove to check on Garrett's whereabouts. Last I knew he had started his evening off with a visit to his friend Adam's place of employment, a nearby local gay bar.

Garrett's newfound friendship with Adam gave me the fucking creeps. Adam gave me eerie vibes, and I just didn't want to be around him. But I was forced to knock on his front door that night. Something about him was off; my gut feelings told me so. Adam said he left Garrett at a strip bar with some gay guys they met earlier that night. Frantic by morning, I dialed Garrett's office. To my surprise, he answered the call, promising to explain everything over dinner. Once home, Garrett admitted to spending the night with a few dudes he had met, because he was too drunk to drive. I smelled a rat. In the back of my mind, I wondered if my husband was gay or bisexual

It would definitely explain some of his behaviors and self-loathing.

Our sex life suffered from that point on. I just didn't trust him. Still, I continued onward, caring for our child, while struggling with my day-to-day responsibilities. There were moments of humor. I'll never forget when I found my little boy playing war in the backyard. I couldn't believe it; my baby had his father's dirty jockstrap wrapped around his little face. He thought he was wearing a gas mask. Gross! God only knows the toxic smell he had endured that afternoon.

On December 9, 1995, Connor, a beautiful, angelic child, was born to this world. When Ryan laid his eyes on his newborn brother, he cried, "Send him back! Send him back to wherever he came from!" I laughed, thinking how hard it was to push his brother's head out of my vagina. There was no way in hell he was going back in. Not long after, I was forced to look for additional work; money was so damn tight back then. My good friend, Fatima, and I decided to start a home-cleaning service. I threw an ad in the newspaper, and within twenty-four hours we had our first call. Awesome, our first call—an older man who needed his house cleaned.

Okay, here's the catch: he wanted us to wear high heels when we vacuumed. A rather odd request, so I called Fatima to get her opinion. She laughed, thinking he was a bit of a weirdo, but I convinced her it would be fine. Really, what was the harm in it? When I called him back, he was elated that we had agreed to the heels. But as I was getting his address and setting the time for the service, he said, "FYI, I just want you to know I am a nudist, and I hope you gals won't have a problem when I am walking around naked as you're vacuuming." WTF? Hell, yes, I had a problem with that. I hung up on the creep. That was the beginning and the end of Bee Cleaning Services.

Connor hadn't even turned one when I discovered Garrett was back to his cheating ways. As I passed by my husband's suitcase that he was packing for an out-of-town business meeting, I noticed a couple of unopened condom packages. I decided to zip my lips, say nothing, and investigate for more evidence after he left. In the trunk of his car, I discovered a bundle of well-worn love notes from Janice. His lover was a local artist almost fifteen years my senior. That weekend, I went to her door early to surprise her, but what surprised me even more were her hairy armpits. I've never really understood why a woman would think it's pretty to have a bush of hair hanging out under there.

She said she was sorry, blah, blah, blah, in her English accent. It was just another sales pitch, but I wasn't buying it. We didn't fight; we shared a simple yet awkward chat over a cup of tea. I left with one photograph of my husband and his lover picnicking on the beach. Definitely I felt like Alice in wonder-what-the-fuck-land. What about that whole "for better or worse" part in our wedding vows? When was it going to get better? Thank God, my dad opened an Irish pub, and I began working as a bartender-manager. It took my mind off my awful marriage.

Seriously, not every marriage affected by infidelity can—or should—be saved, including ours. Grateful for my boys, and the fact that I'd graduated college just one week before my thirtieth birthday, I threw myself into my new job. God must have had a plan in mind for me, because just then, two men entered my life. Both were typical New Yorkers. You know the type, strong accents, very direct, the type of men who loved to chase things, especially women. Jason and Marcus, roommates, entered the pub to look for work. They were both handsome and gregarious; I hired them on the spot. They hit me with the good cop (Marcus)–bad cop (Jason) approach, and it worked.

Sure, they had Irish roots, but it was their humor, fast talking, and looks that got them behind the bar. Truthfully, I enjoyed the attention, and Jason, a natural comedian, was total eye candy. Years later, my father said that at first sight, both of these guys made him feel uneasy. Definitely it was his father-knows-best protective instincts coming out. Pressure continued to build at home until one fateful day, a work associate told me the heart-wrenching truth: Garrett was known all over town as a huge cokehead. The news didn't just stop there. My suspicions had been confirmed: Garrett had a gay lover. I was his beard. What a liar he was, and I a fool. It was at this point I gave up on our marriage.

As soon as my guard went down, the wolves came closer and closer. It was impossible to ignore my physical attraction to Jason. He could be so charming, cutely flirtatious. Why, I hadn't felt pretty in years. I'll never forget our first kiss. We were walking toward my car— he needed a ride home—when wham! Jason shoved me into a breezeway as he pushed his whole body against mine. Our kiss was mindless, untethered, and above all, gloriously spontaneous. Garrett who?

Deep down, I knew that the only way out of my marriage was if I was the one who was unfaithful. We were both miserable not being true to ourselves. Garrett became enraged when he discovered the affair. That's when he punched me in the head from behind. This landed him in jail. He was picked up on charges of domestic abuse and possession of drug paraphernalia. Well, that was a wrap— our marriage and almost-ten-year relationship was over. It was bittersweet, since two beautiful boys had come from such a dysfunctional relationship. Jason was heaven-sent, in my life solely to save me from continuing my future with Garrett—not to mention to teach me about desire and the consequences of our choices in life.

Finally, I divorced Garrett and then took a much needed vacation to visit Jason, who had moved back to

New York. If I had to equate Jason's looks to a doll, he would have been like a Ken doll, but hotter, much hotter. Think underwear model—tall, athletic, chiseled, with a devious smile. The kind of guy you don't marry—you know, the bad-boy type who is better experienced in small healthy doses. Our short encounter was filled with dangerous sex—from subway stations to hot showers. I was able to escape my reality, even if it was just for a little while. With Jason I felt the throes of passion but not inner peace. To this day, I am not even sure if it's truly possible to have both passion and peace at the same time.

At least when I am old and gray, I will have those big, bold, and bright memories. I can roll back the memory rolodex to Jason, who was most definitely Godiva-chocolaty goodness, and that's all I have to say about that. Okay, beyond the great sex, I struggled with my decision to be unfaithful to my husband. I didn't understand that there were different ways to be unfaithful, both to the person one commits to and to oneself. I mean, the act of forgiving me was so much harder than forgiving Garrett.

What happened to my high standards of being a faithful wife? Was it somehow okay for me to cheat because he had done it numerous times with both men and women? I hurt myself when I cheated, because I broke the promise I made in front of God to be a faithful wife. What was left was a tremendous amount of guilt that followed me around for years and years, till I forgave myself and released the pain.

Chapter 6:

THE DEVIL'S
WAITING ROOM

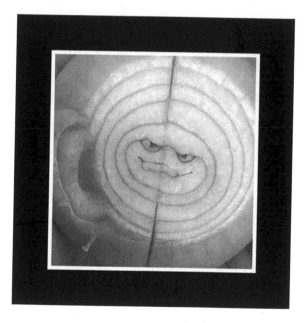

*"A woman's chastity consists, like an onion,
of a series of coats."*
Nathaniel Hawthorne

Leaving Garrett with the house and most of our belongings was surprisingly easy. I was running toward the unknown, but it looked a hell of a lot better than my past.

The move was hectic; I rented a U-Haul truck. I was a one-woman moving company until Marcus, Jason's old roommate, showed up and offered to help me. He had just returned from a trip up north after breaking up with his cheating ex-fiancée. Honest to God, I wasn't really attracted to Marcus; he was a bit overweight and seemed unsure of himself.

What he did have in his arsenal was a pair of the most beautiful pale-blue eyes I had ever seen. They were surrounded by long dark eyelashes that made his eyes look even bluer. I had heard that the eyes are the windows to the soul, so I gave him a chance, believing that with those incredible, unearthly eyes, he must be a real saint. Our relationship began out of a sincere friendship; he really was a nice guy. What he liked about me was my ability to put the needs of others first. Marcus was six foot with a handsome face. So I dusted off my heart and gave it away again…too quickly, of course.

To tell the truth, my new boyfriend wasn't the sharpest knife in the drawer, if you know what I mean. On our first date, he tried to set me up with another man, believing I wasn't into him. I guess, some guys are just clueless when it comes to women. At least he took the initiative to plant a good-night kiss on my lips—awkward, but sweet at the same time. With Marcus, there were not the same sparks flying as when I was with Jason, but it was more of a slow simmer. Certainly, I didn't want to get burned again. But what I did like was Marcus's heart of gold around my two little boys.

The weird thing was, the more time I spent with Marcus, the more confident I became. In his company, all my senses were enhanced—touch, sight, sound; everything became that much more intense. Boy oh, boy, he lavished his time and attention on me. And he really did remind me of my Donnie Osmond doll. So much so, I asked him to dress like Donnie on Halloween. I, of course, dressed like seventies Barbie. Marcus said I was the most stunning, head-turning woman whom he had ever known, and oddly, I believed him. My whole life I had struggled with my looks, feeling my personality far outweighed my exterior. The weird thing was I secretly loved all of this newfound attention.

But still I had to deal with my ex, Garrett, since he was the father of the boys. And it didn't take long till Janice moved in with him. They married and quickly divorced. What did she think was going to happen? Garrett hadn't stopped using drugs and alcohol. Right from the beginning of the separation, I had issues with Garrett neglecting our sons. After repeated warnings, the Department of Children and Family Services became involved. Unknowingly, I was about to get a blast from my past. I was waiting patiently in DCF's waiting room to speak to a caseworker. I couldn't believe my eyes— Stephanie was walking toward me, introducing herself to me as if we had never met before.

Are you kidding me? She was my younger son's new caseworker. Was she out of her mind? Pretending not to know me in front of her coworkers! Somewhere deep inside of me, from the depths of my soul, I began to yell, "She can't be our family caseworker, because she gave my ex-husband a blow job!" Call it karma. But my gut reaction was to shame her as she had shamed me and my family. She brought it on herself. Really, why would she have even agreed to accept my son's case? Long story short, we were assigned a new caseworker, and after that I had no more issues with the physical care of the boys.

As time went by, Marcus continued to woo me. He perched me high on a pedestal. Yeah, I'm not sure if I told you, but my name, Fiona, means 'the fair one.' My mother named me during her pregnancy; she must have had a premonition that I would have more Nordic than Irish looks. I am five foot ten with light-blue eyes, fair skin, and blond hair, which got blonder as I got older, with a little help from bleach. Really and truly, it was so hard to resist Marcus. He was very charming when he wanted something, and he had his eyes set on me. Although, my parents were opposed to him moving in with the children and me so quickly; they wanted me to have more time for myself. But I was in love for what I felt was the first time in my life.

Somewhere between Marcus's late teens and early twenties, his parents had been divorced. Supposedly, his father had a mistress for much of their marriage. His mother, Sheryl, was so devastated that she divorced her husband and then up and moved to Florida. I felt like Marcus may have been emotionally damaged from this experience, but overall he seemed well-adjusted. What I didn't like was his mother, an intensely cold woman in both appearance and manner. I would equate Sheryl's appearance in my life to gray skies foreshadowing a severe storm. There is no doubt in my mind that I had made contact with a venomous snake. Even Marcus found his mother to be overbearing and intrusive.

From the moment he shared his past, I began to sympathize with my boyfriend's childhood. In a sense, he was a prisoner to the pain of his parents' divorce, which to him was intolerable. His problem was that he couldn't forget the trauma. We can never really run away from ourselves. I naïvely believed that my love could somehow help heal Marcus's pain. If only I could help his soul crawl out from its hiding place. It was obvious; Marcus had an unresolved need for attention, affection, and praise. Still I believed, we were a match made in heaven, since I am empathetic and sympathetic, and I always put others before me.

One thing's for sure, I definitely wasn't a gold digger. My new boyfriend barely survived on the commission he made as a real estate agent. Money, no money, it didn't matter to me, Marcus had won my heart. I guess, looking back, I fell head over heels from the moment I believed I could trust him in the caretaker role for both the boys and me. I had just started teaching when field day rolled around; I remember cheering on the sidelines for my class while they struggled to win at tug of war. During that game, something hit my lower leg; I believed it was a loose stone since it didn't sting like a bug bite. As the weekend unfolded, the pain in my leg became more intense; my calf felt like it was burning. An itchy pimple appeared, leaking yellowish pus.

On Sunday, Marcus insisted I go to the emergency room. I was really surprised when the doctor informed us that I had been bitten by a brown recluse spider, and its venom had caused severe tissue damage. Throughout this stressful ordeal, my boyfriend was my rock. Kindly, he slept by my side during my hospital stay, making sure I was comfortable, cared for, and loved. After the first surgery, I returned to teaching but the infection had spread and forced me to return to the hospital for a second operation. Sure, I became a bit depressed, but overall I felt really lucky to have such an empathic man in my life.

Teaching was a great career, but one that couldn't support my family, so I became a real estate agent. Sheryl trained me, and soon I was able to pay off my entire student loan with the sale of a million-dollar property. It would have taken years to pay off my debt if I had remained a teacher. Although Sheryl was one of the best agents in town, I found her a difficult person to work under and quickly broke away on my own. Within a year, my only sister, Deirdre, decided to join me in real estate. Around this time, Marcus had an unexpected run-in with my ex, Garrett. Tempers flared. Granted, both men had had too much to drink that night.

Looking back, I believe Marcus wanted to defend me, my honor. It came down to Garrett's past physical abuse and Marcus trying to look noble in front of me. Guess what—it worked. Garrett became cowardly, refusing to fight back when a man was on the other side. I actually loved this moment, this memory. Sometimes the winding road toward marriage is too predetermined. We meet, date, fall in love, and eventually we marry. But what of all those in-between moments to be savored? There are times in your life when your values or morals are threatened, leading to choices that can become game changers in your destiny.

Two of my in-between memories were with newfound friends, Darla and Keith. Every couple wants to have other couples to hang with. You know what I mean, right? These two memories left their mark indelibly on my subconscious. If I was to avoid inner tragedy, I was going to be forced to make some decisions on friendship. Avoiding the decision left me for a while teetering on the edge of disaster, spiritually speaking, of course. One weekend, all four of us attended a local rave. Dancing, techno music, and yes, drugs. With Jason and Marcus, I tried cocaine and ecstasy for the first time.

No lie, we had an amazing time and lots of laughs. Keith suggested we head to their house for more drinks. Within an hour, Darla and I were quickly lost in girl talk. Seriously, it took a while before we noticed that our guys had slipped off into another room. Hearing their voices in

Keith's office, I gently pushed the partially closed door open. Straight ahead, flashing on their computer screen, was a woman lying on her back, her legs spread-eagled, completely naked. The camera gradually moved in for a close-up shot of this woman's unshaven vagina. I was repulsed.

My focus shifted toward Marcus's face as I heard a faint voice getting louder and louder. It was Keith, repeating the words, "Doesn't my baby look great?" Astonished, I looked at Darla, then the computer screen, back and forth while hearing Keith's voice. Then a face appeared on screen, I was utterly gobsmacked—it was Darla posing provocatively on that video. Just then Marcus said, "Darla never looked so good." What did he just say? Instantly, my face became flushed. This was definitely a sign that something wasn't right with my guy! I had landed in a bizarre world and was in total disbelief. Surreal as this experience was, I decided to ignore the evening and give our new friends an opportunity to redeem themselves.

Friendships rarely start out as bad, but over time, it became apparent that our new friends were toxic.

Usually while under the influence of alcohol, Keith and Darla would suggest turning up the heat. It seemed this promiscuous couple always wanted to get us naked, but I have a strict clothing policy with friends! They would ask if we wanted to play strip poker or, if we preferred, we could go skinny-dipping in their pool. I never took the plunge (pun intended), despite their many valiant attempts. I would always smile, cringe sheepishly, and decline to undress. Why couldn't I see that this promiscuous couple was leading us toward erotica under the guise of friendship?

By far my most scandalous memory of them is the night Darla and Keith asked us to go to a local club's swingers' night. They told us how much fun it was to indulge in a little voyeurism. They had been there previously. Looking to ignite my rebellious side, I naïvely agreed. Clearly, I wasn't thinking. I was utterly unprepared for what I was about to witness. The swingers' club was in plain view, and let's faces it; this nightclub was designed to remove all inhibitions. I remember the first face I saw as we entered was the bouncer. A huge muscular guy dressed in black, with a deep stare that penetrated my soul. He guarded the door. The highest priority was given to friends of his, couples, and attractive women. Single men were not allowed inside.

After entering the club through the main door, we took a sharp right and bam, straight ahead was a shocking scene. Rapidly, my eyes went wide, and my heart rate increased. There in front of me was a billiards table with a naked woman sprawled across it. A small crowd had gathered, chatting and watching the show. A chill went up my spine as I witnessed the woman in the center of the threesome allowing two men to suck on her nipples, licking her body as they fingered her. I felt a mild sting in my eyes. The sting became stronger as I looked around the room. My body went numb. No matter where I looked, there was more flesh, more deviant behavior. My eyes were as sensitive as if I had just chopped onions.

Marcus and Keith suggested we just have one drink. Darla headed off toward the dance floor. There I stood, knee-deep in people, when a stranger suddenly, yet smoothly, appeared directly in front of me. Excitedly, he said he knew who I was. He had a smug look on his face when he asked why I was there. Obviously he assumed

I was there to indulge in sensual pleasures. He told me he was celebrating his anniversary with his wife. I asked where she was, and he tilted his head and right shoulder behind him, allowing me to see his wife. There she was, half-naked, sitting on a barstool, receiving cunnilingus from a stranger. Her husband stood in a self-satisfied manner, but I looked in horror, seeing a long line of both men and women eagerly waiting to give her oral. Talk about a romantic anniversary, right?

At that moment this man seemed like a cat, purring at my feet. I was terrified in his presence, because he looked like a very hungry cat who also wanted something or someone to eat. Luckily, Marcus swooped in like Little Bunny Foo-Foo, ready to bop this guy on his head. Truly, I felt like an innocent field mouse in this man's presence. It was at moments like this one when Marcus was sowing the seeds of my love. Marcus loved seeing himself through my eyes, as my hero. We both felt the high from falling in love; it felt like the most wonderful drug imaginable. It definitely blinded us to our own faults and imperfections.

Keith found us a table near the dance floor. I noticed a woman giving a man a hand job at the bar. Nearby our table were quite a few elderly women, wearing only men's suit jackets, high heels, and no panties. Desperate for a break, I excused myself to go to the bathroom, where my eyes collided with lesbians stimulating each other. There was nowhere to hide, so I returned to our table. It didn't take long until Darla dragged me to the dance floor. But within moments, she was hot and heavy with a stripper! That was it for me. Game over.

Why is each image burned forever into my memory? It's not like I want to remember that evening. But I had to tell someone, it was eating me up inside. The next morning I asked my brother Brian if he could keep a secret. I'd explode if I didn't spill my guts.

After listening to my story, my brother looked intently at me and asked, "Why in hell were you in the devil's waiting room?"

His words just lingered in the air. Was he right? Had my curiosity finally gotten the better of me? Thinking back, I realized that the bouncer was guarding the gates of hell, and there was a lot of steam coming from almost everyone's crotch. I don't believe I saw a single halo in that sex club filled with debauchery.

Can I play devil's advocate? No, and I am not going to pretend I can. My biggest mistake was not leaving sooner. I am not going to say that everyone had invisible horns sticking out the sides of their foreheads, but there is a devil inside of us all. After that evening I decided to hold on tightly to my integrity. I never returned to that club, and I moved away from that toxic friendship. It wasn't just this one incident that pushed me away from Keith and Darla; it was the accumulation of many uncomfortable moments. Time is precious, and I didn't want any more of my time to slip away in their company. Their illicit behavior led to adultery, which ultimately destroyed their marriage. So I ask, as Publilius Syrus did, *"What is left when honor is lost?"*

Chapter 7:

WHEN IN ROME

"All we have to do is to peel the shrines like an onion, and we will be with the king himself."
—Howard Carter

Do you know I said "I do" to living together before I said "I do" to a marriage proposal? Both times. But unlike in my first marriage, Marcus and my transition from shacking up to tying the knot was seamless. I finally met my best friend, someone I could trust and confide in, someone whom I loved and believed loved me back. Marriage for Marcus was more time-sensitive. Having never been married, he wanted a family. We had dated for about a year and a half when Marcus popped the question. The guy of my dreams surprised me with an unforgettable retreat in one of the world's most beautiful hotels.

Late on a Friday afternoon, we checked into a pristine suite at the Ritz-Carlton in Naples, Florida. No question, Marcus knew how to set newer and higher standards in the romance department. Our room opened up to a balcony with dazzling views of the Gulf of Mexico. It started to rain as we stepped outside with our glasses of Dom Pérignon to witness the breathtaking views. That rain washed out Marcus's plans for us to take a romantic sunset walk on the beach after dinner. He seemed genuinely disappointed about the rain. We began to savor sophisticated appetizers served by impeccable waiters.

Marcus spared no expense on our exceptional five-star meals; he ordered the fresh sea bass, and I enjoyed the tender bison. To top things off, we flirtatiously shared chocolate fondant with ice cream, courtesy of the pastry chef.

Nonetheless, Marcus just couldn't let the rain thing go. He said, "It's just a little rain, right? We could still go for a walk." Was he kidding? It was a downpour. Besides, I was all dressed up, wearing a brand-new dress.

As we were waiting for the bill, Marcus seemed nervous, fidgeting around in his pocket. All of a sudden, he pulled out a ring box, dark blue with gold trim and a push button on the front. He turned toward me, already down on one knee, and whispered, "Marry me, Fiona. I want you to be my wife." It was so unexpected; I was in shock. He placed the stunning two-carat diamond ring on my finger before I could even answer. Tears of happiness rolled down my face as I whispered yes. Honestly, at that very moment, I thought my life couldn't get any happier.

I don't know about you, but our engagement made us feel as if we were the center of the universe. Nothing felt better than our love as we began to plan and prepare for our upcoming nuptials. And yes, yes, yes, I did feel guilty planning a second wedding, but it was Marcus's first, so I took a wedding mulligan on my first marriage. But really, I didn't want to cheat the man I loved out of the wedding experience.

Since we needed to perfect our first dance as a married couple for our big day, I arranged for private dance lessons. But from the moment we stepped inside the Fred Astaire dance studio, I began to feel how nervous Marcus had become. Normally, he would have moved mountains for my happiness, but at that moment he looked totally uncomfortable. Thank God our professional dance instructor was patient with us. He got us working on our waltz moves immediately.

Truth be told, Marcus was a bit of a homophobe, and he believed that all male dancers, especially male dance instructors, were gay. I told him it was a myth that dancing somehow could turn a straight man gay. But as luck would have it, our dance instructor that evening happened to be gay. Marcus's nerves made our waltz look anything but elegant, so our instructor grabbed Marcus by the waist to teach him to dance. Marcus had to take the submissive role and be led through the moves. God, I only wished I had a camera. I could see how stupid Marcus felt. As long as I live, I'll never forget hearing "Left box turn, right box turn." Needless to say, Marcus refused to attend any more lessons. Thus our first dance as a married couple looked more like we were dancing at prom.

How could I not be head over heels in love with Marcus? He had all the goods. He was Irish American, Catholic, conservative, and family-oriented (or at least great with my sons), and I adored him. Really, he was amazeballs! Did I mention he was building us a dream house? Honestly, I had no expectations of wealth when I was growing up, but each and every day my dreams were becoming my reality, far exceeding anything I had hoped for. Life had become an adventure with Marcus, and we both felt the strong waves of love and passion.

Finally I'd found true love. We were to be married in the month of November, on a yacht. I never tired of

Marcus telling me that I was "the one" for whom he had been waiting his entire life. It's no secret—I absolutely loved every minute of being spoiled. But as the big day approached, I began to battle nerves. Hidden fears surfaced, and I woke up at three o'clock in the morning in the grips of an awful anxiety attack. Shaky, sweaty, and scared, my body was covered in what looked like welts. Not again! Damned if I was going to have another hideous skin reaction on my wedding day.

Yet again, my hero, Marcus, rushed me to the closest emergency room. I was suffering from another allergic reaction. This time, I was having a severe attack of hives. A quick and painless adrenaline injection was all I needed, not once but two nights in a row. But the second night, my fiancé refused to drive me to the ER—red flag—he was exhausted. The hives disappeared just in time for the wedding. I sighed in relief. I just didn't want to disappoint my guy, since he placed so much on value on physical appearance. Our ship captain performed the marriage ceremony on the yacht on the Gulf of Mexico.

It may have been our big day, but I wanted a family wedding so that the boys didn't feel left out. I will admit that my favorite part of that day was listening to Marcus repeat his vows. "I, Marcus, take you, Fiona, to be my lawfully wedded wife, knowing in my heart that you will be my constant friend, my faithful partner in life, and my one true love. On this special day I affirm to you in the presence of God, family, and our friends my sacred promise to stay by your side as your faithful husband in sickness and in health, in joy and in sorrow, as well through the good times and the bad. I further promise to love you without reservation, honor and respect you, provide for your needs as best I can, protect you in times of distress, grow with you in mind and spirit, and always be open and honest with you."

Marcus made that vow to me and also to each child as their new stepfather. He bestowed on each child a lapel pin with three linked rings, symbolizing the blending of our family. There wasn't a dry eye on deck. Of course, my family was particularly sensitive to the meaning of this occasion for my young sons; they had been through so much already. The next thing I remember is the captain turning us around and saying, "Ladies and gentlemen, I present to you Mr. and Mrs...."

From that point on it was the typical stuff—greeting guests in the reception line, the cocktail hour, photographs—minus the ant bites. We were on the top deck, watching the dolphins following the boat, when seemingly out of nowhere, my older son started crying. Normally, Ryan was a happy child, but all of a sudden he was distraught over the idea that Marcus might not be right for me, for us. Of course, I consoled my son, letting him know we would both be there for him and his brother. Can you imagine how betrayed I felt to learn, after the honeymoon, that Marcus had roughly grabbed my son that day? He was overheard saying, "You'd better not ruin my day" to my ten-year-old.

Sadly, Ryan was the very first to see Marcus drop his carefully crafted social mask. And it didn't take long before Marcus targeted Ryan. During our entire marriage, he showed signs of jealousy toward my older son. Why did he make a public declaration to love and commit to my boys if, within half an hour, he was solely thinking of himself? But on our wedding day I was blissfully unaware of that situation. I was just so excited after taking the plunge and committing to spending my life with this man. As we left the boat via the gangway, we were met by Scotsmen in traditional Highland dress, playing bagpipes and drums.

Hand in hand, we walked as a family, leading our loved ones toward the reception room. The scene was picture-perfect; the reception room had an ambiance of a Victorian-style gazebo from the exterior. Even Barbie couldn't have imagined a more enchanting resort to marry her true love. But don't forget, Barbie's first choice was never Donnie; he was the one who lavished her with attention and praise. She had her eyes set on Ken, or some physical fun with GI Joe. Surrounded by floor-to-ceiling windows, we enjoyed music throughout the evening, from the harpist, to the DJ, to traditional Irish music played by Noel Kingston.

There was one regret. My new husband got so drunk that he was unable to perform on our wedding night. Again, I feared this might be a sign from above. Was our marriage jinxed within twenty-four hours? I was upset, and it was days into our honeymoon before I could forgive him. Trust me; it was hard to stay mad at this guy

Why, he had planned the most romantic honeymoon in Hawaii—first-class flights, visiting two of the islands, the works. By the time we arrived in Kauai, the garden isle, we started to really connect. Not that we are golf junkies, but we did sell property on golf courses, so were thrilled to have gotten Tiger Woods's autograph on the trip.

What I didn't know then was that as soon as our honeymoon was over, the honeymoon was *over*. Marcus may have been newly married, but he let go of that newlywed glow on the ride home from Hawaii. What my husband wanted was for me to be his perfect mirror image, the idealized version of what he expected his wife to look like, to act like. Since I already had a pretty distorted view of myself, it was easy for Marcus to get away with belittling me. No matter how unreal his expectations were, I was ready, willing, and able to make the necessary improvements to my exterior. I was to maintain the appearance he had fallen in love with—no tattoos, no additional piercings, only stud earrings, no hoops, hair long and blond.

I was being groomed to be his perfect Stepford wife. Remember, as a young girl I stereotyped the ideal female as pretty, blond, and slim. I wanted to look like a Barbie with her perfect body and yes, even her mountainous, hard-plastic breasts. Marcus had a breast fetish—definitely not too little and yet not stripper large. So I decided, with Marcus's push, to enlarge my breasts. Sure, part of me wanted to make my husband happy, but I also wanted to look better in and out of my clothes. We decided saline implants placed under the muscle would look more natural. I remember the doctor recommending, as he was taking my presurgery photographs, I only go as high as a C cup because of my body's thin frame.

Goodness gracious great balls of fire! I swear I am not a wuss, yet the breast surgery left me reeling in physical pain. When I finally saw my doctor, I expressed my regrets in having breast surgery. You can only imagine the shock on my face when the cosmetic surgeon pulled out my before photo and asked, "Why would you want to go back to looking like this?"

I was crushed. How could he use my before photo against me, unless he was trying to humiliate me in front of my husband? My surgeon had a preconceived opinion that small breasts are a weakness or a flaw in a woman's body. Needless to say, I never returned to that doctor again, although I did get another cosmetic surgery—the removal of a slight bump in my nose.

Is it just me, or is everyone trying Botox baby? Both my husband and I tried it to help prevent wrinkles. Yet he became enraged after I tried a lip-plumping injection. He complained that I looked like I'd made out with the vacuum! After I looked in the mirror, I agreed with him. Don't we all have our own little insecurities, stemming from what we perceive as imperfections? But Marcus took it a step too far by using aggressive remarks to mock me and taunt me into removing that bump from my nose. It's really sad that I let my self-worth be governed by him. My husband insidiously began to tear out from under my feet the pedestal he'd put me on. He fluctuated between adoring me completely and devaluing everything: my appearance, my parenting style, my cooking.

Within a year of our honeymoon, I became pregnant unexpectedly. Marcus was thrilled, but his mother seemed less than enthusiastic. For some reason, she didn't approve of us having a child of our own. But I was thirty-two years old and Marcus was thirty-one; we weren't getting any younger. Ryan was not very happy about the pregnancy, but fortunately, when his little sister arrived, he fell madly in love with her. Nieve, born June 10, 2002, was the glue that bonded our family together. I enlisted the nanny services of a dear friend, Fatima, since Marcus wanted me to return to work immediately after our daughter's birth.

It came as quite a surprise to learn that, in having a daughter; I was forced to deal with my own deep-down insecurities. I'm not sure why I was more than a bit nervous about raising a little girl. I guess I was afraid of dumping all my issues on another female. In my mind, it was easier to raise boys, but Nieve was a great baby, a delightful light in all of our lives. After her birth, I became a real estate broker, and we opened our own residential commercial office. All of a sudden, real estate had become all-important to Marcus. And just as the money started rolling in, my husband started repeatedly putting down other people, especially those he felt were inferior and strangers.

I loved acquiring expensive clothes, cars, homes, and trips. I mean, really, who doesn't? But wealth gave Marcus a very strong sense of entitlement. He became demanding and selfish, and he expected special treatment. Marcus's assertiveness was sexy when we first met, whereas now his dominance seemed unattractive. All of his confidence had become arrogance, his self-assuredness made others feel insignificant, and his determination became thoughtlessness. I started to wonder if I really knew who I had married. This man, my spouse and business partner, was intensely competitive, inside and outside of our home.

Other real estate agents found him arrogant, shallow, and very manipulative. His love of money could never be satisfied. On the surface, we had achieved the American dream, but the truth was, our marriage was deteriorating. We had become a team, one of those "spouses selling houses" couples. Our company preferred the in-your-face approach to marketing our team, Finest Realty. Splashed all over town were our images—across brightly colored bus benches to bus wraps on public buses. It worked.

In my husband's eyes, there was no such thing as bad publicity. What mattered was that he was in the public eye. I struggled to become the best team member for our business, family, and marriage. But slowly Marcus's love of money took the joy out of our work and our home life. The building of our six-thousand-square-foot commercial office was just a way to emulate RE/MAX or Coldwell Banker offices. He envied wealthier agents and offices. In order to maintain his inflated self-image, he constantly rented limos and drank Cristal. Marcus cared more about appearances than substance in our marriage.

Without a doubt, I always loved my husband, despite his dark side. We were both pursuing our careers, but for two different reasons: he wanted status, and I wanted security. There was even a point when Marcus offered to adopt both boys, but Garrett firmly refused. We survived many years by diving into work or vacationing, which included gambling. Prior to my marriage to Marcus, I had never set foot in a casino. Being married to a gambler probably doubled my chances of becoming addicted to gambling. I must admit it was fun to play cards, slots, and roulette, until we faced bills upward of $12,000 a week.

Still there was one vacation memory, I cherished. It was a very romantic trip with my spouse to Rome

Italy. We stayed at a five-star hotel in Rome with a lavish room and private butler. Marcus and I walked St. Peter's Square, which borders the Vatican. I was in awe of the priceless pictures, mosaics, statues, and altars. One thing I try to do on every trip is to light candles for deceased loved ones in any church or chapel I visit. As I was lighting candles, I noticed that there was an opening in a nearby confession booth. When in Rome, do as the Romans do, right? I headed inside a small enclosed booth for the sacrament of penance.

It was supposed to be a once-in-a-lifetime experience—reconciling my sins in such a holy place. As soon as the priest drew back the curtain, he asked me where I was from, if I was married, and whether I had been married in a Catholic church. I told him, "Once I was married in a Catholic church, but we divorced, and I was remarried on a yacht by the boat's captain." I swear I heard that priest fall over when I mentioned the word captain. His voice changed as he told me he would no longer be listening to my confession. He said I had sinned and needed an annulment. The validity of my current marriage was at stake.

Chapter 8:

POLICE SURVEILLANCE

"Like the layers of an onion, under the first lies another, and under that another, and they all make you cry."
—Derrick Jensen

Our ascent toward financial security had been the smoothest of paths, but our love was on shakier ground. Marcus was more of a lone wolf than a teammate in real estate and at home. He constantly attempted to limit my time with friends and family. His inner turmoil turned into deep-seated aggression, shifting from fits of rage to emotionally depriving his wife and children. He wanted to have complete control over our family and business. Over time, Marcus had an ambivalent attitude toward extended family, which didn't help when we were running a family-based business that included both of our mothers, siblings, cousins, aunts, and in-laws.

Each year that passed he withdrew more. If only the whole world could have revolved around him, he might have been happy. Instead of enjoying working with relatives, whom we trusted and loved, he treated them as hired menials. Marcus was forever striving to be the real estate guru, the more experienced Realtor within the marriage, family, and business. It was frustrating working with him as a team selling real estate. It cramped everyone's growth.

Marcus had a long history of alienating colleagues, coworkers, and competitive agents. Employees started quitting, complaining that Marcus was condescending, patronizing, and impatient. Marcus criticized his mother, aunt, and cousin, since they were the first to quit. Once Sheryl voiced her opinions and resigned, she fell from grace with the boss, her son, Marcus. God only knows why I slept with the devil for so long.

I was blinded by love, willing to be misled by someone I believed was good. Even when others started to warn me, I didn't listen because I knew the other, better side of Marcus. After his relatives quit, we withheld some of their commissions, which led to a court case that eventually was resolved through mediation. Looking back, I know I was just as guilty as he was, maybe more, since I was the broker of our company. Oh God! I did the wrong thing for someone I believed was the right guy. I am eternally sorry for hurting his relatives; I alone am accountable for my actions and the pain I caused them.

Not to make excuses, but there was trouble in paradise. Marcus was tormenting everyone in our home with endless, bitter cynicism and displays of disgust

It was difficult to find any middle ground; Marcus was always right, and his actions were totally justified. For the most part, my husband didn't want the added burden of friends. He easily became bored with their lives and their problems. Honestly, it was difficult to listen as he put down our friends and family behind their backs. Why didn't I see this two-faced behavior as a clue to Marcus's true character?

Only now are the most glaring problems in our marriage easy to spot. I was too hung up on fixing Marcus's problems. Sure, it's always easier to see things in retrospect. Forget about encouraging him to heal some of his broken relationships. Any such suggestion would be met with contempt. Who was I in this marriage? I had totally submitted to losing my own identity when I dropped my last name and picked up his. I was reduced to becoming a "hanger" that Marcus dressed with his image of an ideal wife.

Repeatedly, my father said, "Can't you see your husband is obsessed with you? It's like he wants to skin you and wear you." Marcus loved me like a thing, a possession. He absolutely wore me like a new outfit and loved the way I felt on him, like a fine garment. Underneath it all, I refused to believe I was merely arm candy but the love of Marcus's life, troubled as that life may have been. I mean, I didn't know one perfect individual in my life. My world was filled with flawed people who are still worth loving. And then one spring day, I found Connor at the side door with a few superficial cuts. He was complaining of a headache, so I laid him on the couch and gave him some Tylenol, and I tended to his cuts.

Marcus reacted like a caveman, yelling at Connor, "Get the fuck off the couch. Man up, you pussy!" Obviously, Marcus didn't have the patience or understanding it took to be a parent. Connor and Ryan grew up without their biological father and had a stepfather who lacked common sense and manners. Our home was like the school of hard knocks, teaching painful lessons to all who interacted with Marcus. Feeling the need to protect my son, I urged him to shower in order to flee Marcus's wrath. No sooner did my son finish showering than he began to projectile vomit uncontrollably. Marcus screamed, "Bitch, don't make him a mama's boy, just let him sleep it off!"

My motherly instincts took hold. Something was terribly wrong with my child, so I rushed him to a nearby hospital. The emergency room responders started testing my son's reactions to different lights while asking him to relax. Unknown to me, Connor had fallen off the top of a golf cart, hit his head on the street, and had a seizure. The driver was Connor's new friend. He was so scared that he made a quick decision to leave Connor at the door without telling anyone what had happened. After an MRI, CT scans of his brain, and standard X-rays of his head, the doctors discovered a traumatic brain injury.

There was a lot of confusion around the fact that Connor needed to take a life flight alone for immediate surgery in Tampa. But as luck would have it, there was one experienced pediatric neurosurgeon that was willing to treat Connor locally. I was powerless to help my baby boy! Marcus still denies his vicious tirade toward his stepson that evening. My husband often used denial as a defense mechanism, so he didn't have to face his inner demons. Dr. Eskioglu stopped the bleeding, letting Connor escape brain damage and—even worse—death. Every boy needs to know his dad loves him, which is why it was so hurtful to Connor that Garrett didn't show up until a week after surgery.

Then Fatima, our nanny, alerted me to Marcus's day drinking. I was wondering what was interfering with my spouse's ability to work and function on a daily basis. Unfortunately, denial goes hand in hand with alcoholism for both Marcus and me. I had finally crossed the river of denial with regard to my husband's reckless driving, gambling, and compulsive shopping. Since I am a child of an alcoholic, denial ran much deeper. To this day, my mother insists that there was never an issue with my father's drinking. But then why do I remember wanting him to stop drinking, to choose us over the alcohol?

Thank goodness, my father now abstains from drinking alcohol. But as is quite often the case, my father had physically overcome one addiction, only to develop another: gambling. My dad finds that gambling makes him happy; it's a rush. But I ask myself whether the quality of his life is being destroyed by the very thing that is supposed to make him happy. The outcome to all of this was my dysfunctional way of thinking about alcoholism, gambling, and other addictions.

By late fall 2006, Marcus started exhibiting extreme and irrational fears that neighborhood teens were conspiring against him. To say the least, he was paranoid. He distrusted everyone, including his own family. He labored under the delusion that during the wee hours of the morning, young adults were attacking our home. Frustrated by what he perceived as imminent danger to his family, he began pacing the neighborhood with large pellet guns and a baseball bat. Our local neighborhood watch recognized and reported Marcus's suspicious activity. What the hell was he thinking, running down our streets wielding a paintball rifle and dressed in camouflage gear?

My husband's abuse included a systematic pattern of behavior where he withheld all cell phones, pushed, screamed, and forced sleep deprivation on his family. Denying the boys and me of sleep was done by starting arguments at a late hour, turning on all the lights in the house, or bumping our beds intentionally. He woke Ryan, in high school at the time, to watch from our rooftop for invisible intruders. His nightly exploits left us walking around in a fog, unable to think clearly. Obviously

Marcus needed help—his thoughts and behaviors were unhealthy. Since I was worried about his mental state, I set up an appointment for us to meet with a psychiatrist.

Supposedly, the terrifying experiences added up to a diagnosis of bipolar disorder. Treatment of this disorder would include therapy, with drugs to control my husband's shifts in energy, mood, and ability to function. But as weeks turned into months, therapy was not working, and Marcus had little motivation to change. Marcus would hole up in our house, not coming out unless he was stalking me. He started to point the finger and blame me for his pain, believing I was having an affair. Jealous, he began hiding tape recorders in my car, under our bed, and throughout our home. Over and over, Marcus would confront me, with static recordings, insisting he heard a male's voice and the intimate moans of sex.

Did you ever notice that someone who thinks that world is always cheating him is correct? It must be awful to live a life without that amazing feeling of trusting in someone or something. For me, my second marriage was about living up to my moral standards, which included being a faithful wife. Marcus even accused me of masturbating behind the wheel, in front of our children. He must have been deeply disturbed. How could I referee my kid's arguments, navigate through busy streets, and still find the time to masturbate? His accusation was delusional, ludicrous, and yet comical. I was being stalked in my own home; there was no privacy. My husband snooped through e-mails and cell messages and recorded my every move.

Extremely suspicious, Marcus purchased a UV black light to check my panties for evidence of another man's semen. Holy cow, he had watched one too many episodes of *CSI Miami*. The bottom line was my guy was acting like a complete wacko, and when I turned to his psychiatrist, I couldn't get any help. Due to patient-physician privacy rules, I was unable to discuss Marcus's condition. I was very concerned that his antipsychotic drugs weren't helping, and his hallucinations were getting worse. His condition was robbing our children of any normality in their daily lives.

Obviously, I believed Marcus was having a nervous breakdown. For years, Marcus was constantly maxing out our credit cards, and by the time it was over, we were over our heads in debt. Finally, it took law enforcement to break the case, or the reason for my husband's craziness, wide open.

"I just need you to listen," said Officer Watkins as he was about to hit me over the head with the truth. "Did you know your husband, Marcus, called in a personal favor from the head of the local sheriff's office? After said call, the sheriff department set up surveillance on your property over this past weekend." Ridiculously enough, they brought night-vision goggles and set up surveillance cameras aiming directly at my home.

What? I couldn't believe my ears. An undercover spy operation was commenced without my knowledge due to my husband's mental condition. Officer Watkins was shocked that Marcus had Robert Sky's personal number, and even mentioned how unusual it was for a civilian to speak directly to him. Marcus reported suspicious activities with regard to teens terrorizing his family nightly. As the officer described the scene that unfolded the last night of the surveillance, I couldn't help but smile. It must have been one crazy-ass night when

Marcus called the cell phone of one of the undercover officers telling him, "Come here quickly, they're here now!"

But unbeknown to Marcus, because the deputies wanted the element of surprise, they'd arrived earlier than expected. As Marcus was peering through his sports binoculars at invisible intruders, the cops, with their night-vision goggles, were watching him watching no one. Boy, I imagine the sheriff's deputies on duty felt foolish, watching Marcus, a very special, special agent, wasting their time and precious tax dollars. "We would like you to sign a form, consenting to 'Baker Act' your husband," said the officer. He needed my consent to allow for an involuntary examination of Marcus.

After their investigation, they believed my husband could harm himself or others, and either he was a drug user or had a mental illness. I was in utter disbelief. Yet I couldn't bring myself to sign that form to institutionalize Marcus. It was kind of a Catch-22 situation. I loved him, but his unseen illness was alarming. Returning home, I found Marcus barricaded in our bedroom, emotionally absent and lethargic. My spouse had a tumultuous relationship with his mother and an almost nonexistent one with his father. But after Sheryl saw a recent photo of her son, she instantly knew he was abusing drugs again.

On a handful of occasions prior to our marriage, Marcus and I had tried cocaine together. He swore he only used it recreationally and quit completely for the boys and me. My trial and error was attributed to finding out why Garrett loved cocaine more than us. Plain and simple, addictions and dependence ran in both his and my families. What I discovered was that my children meant more to me than any substance ever could. Funny, prior to our wedding, Sheryl never mentioned to me, a woman with two small boys, that her son had a cocaine addiction. Most of his family had been rude as hell to me during this trying time, as I reached out to them for much needed help.

Marcus hit his melting point the morning after my meeting with Officer Watkins. He had a full-blown psychotic episode in front of the children and our neighbors. We had to flee our own home for fear of being further attacked. Sheryl pulled the "blame and bolt" move by picking Marcus up, driving him to a rehab on the east coast of Florida, and blaming his addictions on me. Generously, his parents split the cost of his inpatient care at the Water Shelter, an addiction treatment program in Boca Raton. Marcus's mother believed in the tough-love approach to getting her son a little help, so he would do much better.

But Marcus needed to hit his own rock bottom in order to heal; she couldn't do it for him. As Marcus and Sheryl fled the county, I filed for an injunction for protection against my husband. But it was never served, since he had left the area. My mother-in-law quickly asked for Marcus's Cadillac Escalade to be brought to her condo. It was an odd request, considering all that we were going through at the time. In her eyes, I sabotaged her family's attempts to aid Marcus's sobriety and even wanted Marcus to continue his drug addiction. Still, it wasn't her responsibility to keep her son on the right path. Truly, a person's character lies in their own hands, not in their parents.

I went nuts when I discovered a hoard of porn in Marcus's vehicle. In a frenzy, I taped Misses December, January, February, March, and so on all over the interior of my husband's SUV. As I intended, this bevy of nude beauties was only visible from the bottom of the windows to the floor mats. Boy, I wish I'd been a fly on the wall when Sheryl got a look at her son's porn collection. Really, why did she even need his car at that point? Was there drugs hidden inside it? Although in my defense, when you live with a crazy person, ultimately some of their crazy rubs off on you.

Am I wrong, or is "Thou shalt not steal" one of the Ten Commandments in the Bible? Not to mention it's a crime. But after Marcus left, I discovered that his relatives' missing commissions, the kids' college savings bonds, and over $30,000 of my jewelry had gone toward his three-year drug addiction. Sadly, he even stole from a children's cancer foundation; he used the pledge money for cocaine. His dealer of choice was a sixteen-year-old neighbor in our upstanding gated community. For some unknown reason, he destroyed his own reputation when it seemed like he had everything he always wanted.

At this point, I was certain I wanted a divorce, but Marcus begged me to help him. I tried to block his calls and pleas for support, but he promised he would overcome his illness. It didn't seem real that I could marry two men with addictions to alcohol and cocaine. Was I a coke magnet? My spouse had crossed my line in the sand, that boundary I had set prior to our marriage, and yet I let him come home. What was wrong with me? Now, I realize that making it about me was my first mistake, and not leaving him when he crossed a major boundary was my second.

Yes, I was naïve. Somehow, Marcus sidestepped my anger, wooing me back to him by becoming the man I had first met. He attended a few AA (Alcoholics Anonymous) meetings, yet he firmly refused to attend NA (Narcotics Anonymous) meetings, because he was "not like those crackheads." He had the mind-set of a crazy person still. You know, it's like that saying you can take the rum out of the fruit cake, but you still have the fruit cake. This said, Marcus didn't stay away from alcohol for too long. Why should he? But thank God, eventually everyone sits down to a banquet of consequences.

By the end of that year, we planned a family cruise, which felt like a daunting task. I was worried that the ship's party lifestyle would trigger my husband to fall off the wagon. Should he have put himself in that situation? Probably not. The nightmare began when Marcus sat down to a full table and played blackjack day and night. Gambling on the high seas was a bad bet for us, since he lost almost $15,000 in one week. We argued, but he continued to max out the last of our credit cards. I took a lot of flak as I questioned Marcus for constantly walking around with a pilsner glass filled with cold beer. He insisted he was drinking nonalcoholic beer on tap. It took this dum-dum more than two days to figure out there are not enough teetotalers on board to have kegs of nonalcoholic beer.

Once his secret was out, he went hog-wild, even drinking in front of the children. He woke up using buckets of ice-cold Budweiser beers and spent his time at the casino. After losing, he retired to the bathroom to shomit—shit and vomit at the same time. The kids passed through the bedroom gagging and trying not to throw up. Of course I felt bad for Marcus, but I couldn't focus solely on his alcoholism for too long. I had to take back a piece of my own life, at least for the sake of the children.

No, he really wasn't sorry for his mistakes. Truly, he didn't care about the pain he was causing, pretending to be clean and sober. Marcus was a terrible friend, lover, partner, and father. God! I became bitter and passive-aggressive, and it felt like we were just cohabiting. It was soul crushing to listen as he continued to fake his sobriety date in front of loved ones. Marcus transferred his addiction from alcohol and cocaine to gambling, and finally to an exercise addiction. He became dependent on running, training, and competing in marathons in order to cope with his perceived lack of dopamine in his brain. His compulsive excessive exercise was just another way of dodging and ducking away from any deep emotional attachments.

Chapter 9:

GOD'S CALLING WITH CANCER

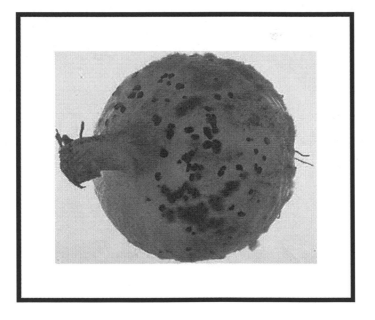

"It's better to be healthy alone than sick with someone else."
—Dr. Phil

The burning truth was we were living with Dr. Jekyll and Mr. Hyde. In public, Marcus was hyperfriendly, but once the cameras were turned off, he was extremely cold, even callous. I fell in love with the bright side of Marcus's personality, but no matter how I begged him, he preferred his dark side. Still, I was in love with my husband, so with a few momentary glimpses of the man I married, I was hooked again. As soon as he had me again, he quickly attempted to gain control of our relationship.

By late 2007, the housing market bubble had burst, forcing us—as well as half of the state—to short sell our beautiful home. We were hit with a double whammy: the loss of our money from Marcus's drug addiction and the housing industry falling apart. No matter what, I had become zealously loyal to my husband. I was his biggest and only cheerleader. My spouse was emotionally wounded. But the more I cared and nurtured, the more he would run. In time, Marcus justified using alcohol and drugs again. He felt I was a burdensome wife. My fantasy of having a healthy marriage had long since died, but I was unwilling to face reality.

Since the public stopped flipping houses, our finances flipped from riches to rags. The luxury vehicles were repossessed, the commercial building was handed back to the bank, and we permanently closed the doors to Finest Realty. Marcus griped and griped. Gone in what seemed like an instant was all the prosperity we had accumulated. But I was about to learn that I had not lost it all, not yet. For it has been said that the real measure of your wealth is how much you'd be worth if you lost all your money. And for me, no truer words have ever been spoken!

Marcus suggested we take separate vacations in July 2009, since we couldn't agree on a family summer holiday. At first, I was afraid that separate vacations meant our lives were going in separate directions. He wanted to visit friends and family in New York with our daughter. And I decided to cash in on a free cruise promotion with my sons, sister, and nephew. We both got a real surprise in June, when I discovered I was pregnant with our second child.

Really, we had no plans to have another child. I didn't want to be pregnant after forty. But God is the giver of life, and we were both genuinely elated about having another baby in the house. By the time the cruise ship docked in Cozumel, I began having what seemed like a very heavy period. That day and into the evening I was convinced that I had miscarried our baby. All it took was a few blood clots and major cramping, and the baby disappeared. The miscarriage was a devastating experience. I felt sad, confused, and alone.

After that we had to move into a rental. But within months, we were forced to move again, unable to afford the rent. Most of the burden of physically packing and moving our family fell on my back. It was grueling work. Weary, I needed to rest, and I accepted Sheryl's offer to use her condo at a discounted rental rate. In retrospect, I should have suspected my monster-in-law, a master in the art of war, was plotting to destroy my marriage to her son. Definitely, Sheryl believed in keeping her friends and enemies close, and her daughter-in-law even closer.

Certainly her intentions were not pure. She was unable to view her son as the problem; she completely blamed me for all of his mistakes. Clearly, I didn't think this through, but I was financially, mentally, and physically falling apart. Between work and family, finding the time for my health came last. For well over a year, I noticed a dark, tar-colored blood in my stool. My family physician had referred me to Dr. Keith to get a colonoscopy in January. We were financially strapped, so I waited eleven months before actually making an appointment.

On the morning of the colonoscopy, I remember I was thumbing through a gossip magazine, when a rather large woman sat down next to me. Instantly, she let out one of the loudest farts ever—you know, something that could have been recorded in the *Guinness Book of World Records*. No one in that waiting room acknowledged that noise, yet I found it hilarious. I felt like Christopher Columbus discovering somewhere new. The one place anyone could pass gas safely: the gastroenterologist's office. Thank God for the comic relief during that stressful moment.

What I wasn't prepared for was the wake-up call of my life given to me on December 14, 2009, after coming out of anesthesia. Still groggy and foggy-headed, my doctor informed me that I had stage III colon cancer, with a 40 percent chance of survival

"Why worry about a little blood on the toilet paper? I'm sure it's just hemorrhoids," I had repeatedly said to myself for over a year. And oh my God, I should not have self-diagnosed my illness; it just wasn't a great substitute for professional medical advice. Shock ran through my body that morning. Marcus was standing by my side, but his soul was filled with rage, intensely angry for having to rearrange his schedule that day.

Yeah, well, you know, the large hole that we spent years trying to climb out of had just become a sixty-foot-wide sinkhole. All I knew is I needed him, but whenever I had moved toward him emotionally in the past, he always pulled away. I guess our relationship was sort of a push-pull dance, full of highs but many more lows. I was there when he needed my time, attention, and love during his battle against drug addiction. But while I gave myself fully to him, I neglected my own needs, including my health.

After the procedure, I halfheartedly agreed when Marcus suggested breakfast with Sheryl and her husband. Marcus always felt more powerful when he was in control, but I wished he had been capable of putting himself in my shoes. He would have realized I needed my loved ones then more than ever. Not surprisingly, he made everything about him and what he wanted. I didn't realize there was something innately wrong with me—I did not love myself enough to voice my opinion. I needed to speak my truth, not for Marcus, but for me and my health—mind, body, and soul.

At that point in my life, I had no real connection to my true self. Thank goodness, breakfast was short. It seemed surreal to be hugged by those who didn't really care for me. Deep down, I was looking for Marcus to shield and protect me, like the man I fell in love with when we first dated.

I didn't want to hurt my parents' feelings by breaking the news of my life-threatening condition. I just knew, my mother didn't take the news well. She was a hope hospice nurse and felt guilty for not pushing me harder to get the colonoscopy sooner. I reminded her that I was solely responsible for my actions and inactions. Still, I was terrified to tell my kids, to see the looks on their faces and witness the consequences of my not seeking treatment earlier.

Why didn't I realize that the earlier the stage at diagnosis, the higher the chance of survival? I told my oldest, Ryan, over the phone, since he was attending Hope College in Michigan. Instantly, he broke down crying and decided to move back to Florida. It is never a pleasant task breaking bad news to one's children, but I feared the emotional toll the news would take on them. Marcus told the two youngest after school, thinking it was best to share the news face-to-face.

When they saw me, they ran to me, keenly aware of my facial expressions as I assured them everything would be all right. I always wanted to protect my children from the pain that life could bring, hoping their childhood would be carefree and filled with joy. We spent the day discussing ways to regain my health and help the children during this time. What I need to do was focus on the fight ahead and not the fright associated with the unknown. The weird thing is certain types of cancer, like colorectal cancer, run in some families, but there was no family history in ours. I had been craving and chewing on ice for months, which meant I was anemic. Except for being anemic and having a small amount of blood in my stool, I felt healthy.

I was only forty-one years old. I didn't smoke and I wasn't overweight, so I was an unlikely candidate for anal cancer. Remember my aunt Martha? She was also waging war against cancer at that time. Her husband had survived lung cancer, but Martha unfortunately succumbed to multiple myeloma.

From the moment my husband heard of my diagnosis, he chose to sleep in a separate bedroom. I was heartbroken. Can you blame me? He insisted I would sleep better alone. I should have seen this as a red flag, right? Please, of course it felt like he was abandoning me, just when I needed him most. Sure on and off, throughout our marriage there was some warmth or tenderness. I mean, how else would we have made it almost ten years.

But my concerns lies with the times we made love, Marcus lacked an interest in foreplay, going straight to dry penetration. Natural lubrication diminished his pleasure; he preferred sex raw, rough, and without emotional connection. Sex with Marcus was so impersonal and emotionless, and it was usually more fulfilling for him than me.

No doubt, I am a girly-girl who wanted to make love. You know—passionate, romantic, and intimate moments, rather than just having sex. Marcus didn't want a deeper connection; he just wanted to feel good by using my body to masturbate. Why were our souls drawn together if we could not emotionally and physically express love? Marcus screamed at me many times that the cancer was God's way of punishing me for not being a good wife. There were so many times he would verbally kick me in the guts just for good measure, to make sure I knew everything wrong with him, and us, was my fault.

Other times, Marcus invoked the silent treatment as a way of getting back at me throughout our marriage. Sometimes, there was no explanation for this treatment. It was frustrating, since it would go on for hours, days, and sometimes weeks. Maybe he feared losing me to death, since he relied on me for attention and support. But instead of communicating his fears, he sulked and showed indifference. I'll be the first to admit we had lived above our means, and now our business was ruined, and our credit was destroyed. But in the wake of my illness, Marcus insisted we file for bankruptcy. After the cancer diagnosis, most of my time was filled with appointments for CT scans, PET scans, and MRIs. And it didn't take long till my oncologist confirmed the biopsy was indeed cancer.

Surgery was recommended as the most effective treatment for removing my tumor. Funny enough, I accepted the cancer as part of my life, more so than other parts, like being a perfectionist. Having high standards, striving for flawlessness, and demanding better from myself led to unhappiness. Putting too much attention into the details, caring about the little things as if they were big things—these added up to one hell of an anal-retentive person. Who said God doesn't have a sense of humor? I thought he was pretty funny giving anal cancer to someone as anal as me. Since chemo demands many needles, I had a port implanted. It is easier to access the port leading straight to one's heart. I forged forward, not wanting to be a victim of cancer but a survivor of cancer.

I met with my radiation oncologist, who informed me that prior to surgery, I would be receiving radiation therapy combined with chemotherapy. Shrinking the tumor was the first priority. He explained the side effects of the radiation therapy, which would include fatigue, loss of appetite, decreased blood count, and fertility problems. If I hadn't had a miscarriage, I would have avoided chemotherapy and radiation therapy for the sake of our child. Yet the loss of our child allowed for the cancer treatments. Dr. Brown said, "It will be virtually impossible to conceive after radiation." So I decided, to trust in the lord with all my heart, and not lean on my own understanding, or lack thereof.

Chemo was scary the first time; I truly feared the unknown. The first round of chemo lasted ten weeks, in addition to radiation twice a week. The implanting of the first port had given me MRSA, a potentially dangerous staph infection. It actually reminded me of the recluse spider bite: swollen, red, pus-filled, and extremely painful. In an attempt to save the port, I had to sit for hours in an infection specialist clinic receiving antibiotic intravenously. My particular strain of MRSA was resistant to the first-line antibiotics, so I returned to surgery. I was exhausted after the placement of three ports and two temporary catheters. Talk about feeling like a fuckin' pincushion.

Marcus begged me to find other rides to treatments, because he was tired and bored, and he needed his space. It bugged me that he didn't appear to need me or even want to care for me. Not wanting to put an extra strain on him, I enlisted my father, aunt, and others to help. But his behavior was mind-boggling—he continued to show up at appointments after complaining he didn't want to be there.

I convinced myself Marcus was fighting caregiver stress, as he screamed over and over, "Get the fuck up and carry your fair share of the work around here!" It didn't matter that I was in a pretty fragile state, very weak and often vomiting. Why Marcus, why? You said you'd catch me if I ever fell, and I truly believed you…till I hit the ground. What happened to our marriage vows?

At least he pushed me to attend a colorectal cancer support meeting. Why? One of his clients ran the group. It was all for show. He could kill two birds with one stone: solidify his business relationship and prove he was a doting husband. On a positive note, it was promising to see so many survivors. Still, it didn't take long till Connor started to complain, teary-eyed, about Marcus's emotional abuse. His stepfather didn't realize you can hurt someone without even touching them. I remember saying, "Mommy loves you very much, but my body is too weak to drive."

Of course, my husband's abuse left no physical marks on my children. Yet large scars were definitely left on their hearts, and for this I feel guilty. Without a doubt, we were stuck in purgatory with Marcus, stranded somewhere between heaven and hell. All I can say is my husband had an unbendable will of steel. Really he hated, but projected all of his self-hatred onto his family.

By this time, my kids and I had learned well the lessons of survival; hell hath no fury like Marcus's wrath. Heaven has never seen rage like my spouse's as his love turned to hatred. My family was shocked by the disdain with which Marcus treated me. As they attempted to intervene on behalf of their sick daughter and grandchildren, a masterful cover-up took place, and of course, lies were told. Marcus perceived their questions as criticism. If all of this wasn't enough stress, our daughter Nieve was preparing for her first communion. When Nieve finally received her first Eucharist, I watched proudly from my wheelchair.

Thankfully, Nieve found solace during this time in a friend who had moved part time into our building. But her mother was another issue. Penny was attractive from a distance, but up close she was a real "butter face." You know the type; everything looks great but her face. She was a well-known man-eater and had her eyes on our neighbor, a recently divorced doctor. Maybe I should have worried about the possibility of sexual shenanigans between my husband and Penny, but I was too damn sick.

I'm not sure why, at this point in time Sheryl decided to take an intense interest in her son, Marcus. I must have been stupid to think her newly developed curiosity was authentic. My mother-in-law spent her life building assets, not relationships. Sheryl and I were just two different people; no matter how I tried, she barely tolerated me as her daughter-in-law. During my first round of chemo, I realized Sheryl had become an intrusion on my marriage. I should have remembered that good fences make good neighbors, but of course I forgot Robert Frost's wise words. Yep moving into my mother-in-law's building was a huge mistake; our lives should have been divided in order to keep peace. Sheryl's interference caused many disagreements.

It was during the chapter 7 bankruptcy that Sheryl helped funnel Marcus's commissions back to him. And sure as shit, hiding assets landed her in hot water with the judge, not to mention a steep fine. She also put a newer used luxury SUV in her name, in order for Marcus to avoid disclosing that asset to the trustees. Money was their god, plain and simple.

As soon as radiation and the first round of chemotherapy were complete, we took a cruise. Really, I am not sure how anyone talked me into another cruise after the last nightmarish one. Anyway, the red flags that appeared on that vacation included the exclusion of the boys and me from a family photo, and Marcus's outbursts of anger. What hurt most was Marcus's tirade after losing his hairbrush. He blamed me for moving it and screamed, "You won't need a fucking hairbrush soon. You'll be bald!" His words couldn't be taken back. I had given them power, allowing them to bounce off my heart, echo back in my ears, and cut my soul in half. His thoughtless words cut a sharp knife, dicing an onion.

In my corner, my family celebrated my hair by posting photographs sporting blond wigs on Facebook. It was their way of supporting me, knowing my hair might thin or fall out. They loved me for me, with or without hair. Deep down, I already knew if I lost my hair, all of it, that my husband would no longer find me desirable. In fact, I didn't go bald; fortunately, I just lost some clumps of hair. Yet, my biggest fear was about to come true… it was having an ileostomy bag—a pouch that collects the body's wastes. And of course, I would need one while my colon healed after surgery; still I knew Marcus would reject me because of it.

Can you believe my first surgery date was postponed? Marcus insisted I attend a bankruptcy hearing and put off removing the tumor. Of course, that left my parents furious; they felt my health should have taken priority. Finally, on April 15, 2009, tax day, my surgeon removed the cancerous tumor and some lymph nodes. And then she created an opening in my small intestine, at the end of the ileum. Next, she brought my intestine through my abdominal wall and formed a stoma. Really, I was lucky, the ileostomy was just temporary; at most, I would have it six months. Never will I forget when I woke up after that surgery, screaming in agony. I had the most brutal pains throughout my lower abdomen.

The nurses loaded me up with pain meds and wheeled me off to my private room. I was looking forward to seeing my loved ones. Instantly Mom and Dad rushed to my side, but not Marcus. He was extremely standoffish. In the days that followed my surgery, I had a barrage of visitors. I can't remember much, since I was floating in and out of consciousness. What I do remember was looking at my husband with blurred vision, sitting in the corner, filled with doom and gloom. Then I heard all of my family discussing Ryan's upcoming twenty-first birthday. Really, it was more of a game of "what if" than reality as they discussed a celebration in Las Vegas.

You know the game. "What if we all flew to Las Vegas first class?" "What if we reserved a floor of rooms at the Bellagio?" "What if we danced and gambled all night?" It was a harmless conversation to pass the time and lift everyone's spirits. Then the nurse came in to care for my stoma. Everyone left but Marcus. I could feel his revulsion; it was so profound, I began to feel shame. Later that night, my mom brushed my hair, just as she did when I was young. Both of my parents heard Marcus say, "Why bother brushing her hair? She won't have any soon!" His cruel words almost killed my father.

You know, I half-expected to see my dad blow-up. Marcus had messed with the bull, so I believed he was going to get the horns. But thank God, my father has inner strength and patience. Really, he could have exploded. Still, Marcus's intent to injure me didn't end there. He continued to insult me after I returned home. He began to call me "shit bag." He knew I was sensitive to the ileostomy bag, so he took advantage of the opportunity to hurt me. Something inside of me was dying; he was murdering my soul, inch by inch, with every vicious comment. Like a vampire, Marcus continued to suck the soul right out of me.

The most painful words I have ever heard came running out of his mouth. We were driving toward my two-week postoperative appointment with my surgeon, Dr. Dyke. He was outraged by the conversation in the hospital about celebrating Ryan's twenty-first birthday in Vegas. I assured him it was impossible, especially with my illness. That's when he said it: "You'll be dead by Ryan's birthday!" I couldn't stop crying. No one had ever said I might not make it. My uncontrollable episode of crying lasted all the way through my appointment. When I asked my doctor, she questioned why I believed I was going to die. I said my husband told me, and she gasped. Marcus showed no remorse, became defiant, and gave a halfhearted apology within five minutes of arriving home.

Dr. Dyke did order another PET scan, since she felt something suspicious on my liver during the surgery. I never asked if my health was improving, I just blindly followed the doctor's advice. My PET scan lit up like a Christmas tree. I was told I had bone cancer and less than two years to live. One of the hardest things is to be told you're going to die. No one is ever ready for this news; my doctors said I had less than two years, at most. I kept telling myself to hang in there long enough, I would get better, and all our struggles would have been worth it. We all celebrated Mother's Day with a special brunch on the very boat that Marcus and I had been married on. My family remained mindful of my recent news; they were caring and compassionate. But a few times I looked over at Marcus, only to witness crocodile tears. Instinctively, I knew he was insincere, yet still I hoped he loved me, somewhere deep down. At night, I couldn't sleep and started having anxiety or panic attacks. I pleaded with Marcus to talk to me, comfort me, but he made excuses why I deserved my death sentence. The man I loved mocked me for being a baby whenever I cried about my illness and fear of death.

Why couldn't my husband support me, as I supported him during his struggles with addictions? Did he always lack empathy? Beneath his handsome exterior lurked a dark, heartless soul, seeking to control and abuse me. As I hit what seemed like rock bottom, he pounced on my frailty and exploited my weaknesses to the maximum. I got on my knees, after I realized that God was calling me with cancer. Ryan was turning twenty-one, and I was dying. Hadn't I made a pact with God, just twenty-one years ago? The Lord was just cashing in on my solemn bargain to take my life: I had lived long enough to raise my firstborn son.

Chapter 10:

ABUSED AND ABANDONED

"Love is like an onion soup. A good result requires time, commitment, and some tears."
—Unknown Author

During my first pregnancy, I was scared, and all I could offer God in exchange for his protection was my life. For the Lord was merciful; he never abandoned me, and he never forgot my vow. Even though my husband had made my life a living hell, I wanted to save our marriage and be there for our children. Again, during my time of crisis, I turned to God and cried, "Help me, please, spare my life for the sake of all my children, you can take anything, just let me be there for them!" It wasn't hard to admit—I needed God, right then and there. I trusted him and knew he wouldn't forsake me.

Deep inside of me, there was this spark of heavenly fire, which would lie dormant while things in my life were good. But when faced with profound grief or fear my inner light would burn brighter yet burn out much faster. Using the last bit of my inner strength, my light kindled up, as I pushed for additional testing, since PET scans aren't always 100 percent accurate. The results were a mixed blessing. I had a bone infection, not bone cancer. Yet things with Marcus went from bad to worse. Really, it was a mixed blessing to be brought back from the brink of death. The darkest hour of adversity should have been behind me. I wasn't able to rejoice in the good news for long. Indeed, I was hanging on to by the skin of my teeth, as I allowed someone else to dim my inner light.

Marcus decided I was unworthy, so he abandoned me and the kids. Gleefully, he staged a fight, tormenting and teasing me about my illness. Marcus moved out on Father's Day! Till this very day, my husband tells a tale of being thrown out by his ill wife. But the difference between his position and mine was just a matter of semantics. No matter what the phrasing or terminology, Marcus moved upstairs with his mother, never returning home again. Hiding behind his mother, he repeatedly refused to speak with me or aid in the care of the children.

Instead of losing my cool, I tried to stay calm while reaching out for help. Sheryl screamed at me that Marcus was run-down and filled with fatigue due to my illness. Not exactly grieving for the loss of my marriage, Sheryl offered me rides to chemo, as long as my therapy didn't interfere with her mah-jongg games at the clubhouse. Chemotherapy was necessary for me to live; however, my health had become a low priority. As the mother of

Marcus's child, I would have felt wonderful to have been respected. Many times Sheryl became hysterical, yelling that Marcus and I would never be together again.

After a brutal breakup, Marcus left for…where else? Disney World! Just like the commercials—win a Super Bowl and go to Disney. Maybe Marcus would start a tradition, too. "I just wrecked my marriage today. I'm going to Disney World!" "If your wife has a life-threatening illness, it's definitely time to enjoy the magic of Disney!" This trip was financed by who else-Sheryl. After that long weekend was over, Marcus returned to living with his mother again.

But oddly, days later, a letter arrived from one of the luxury Disney resorts confirming the booking on November 10, 2010, our ten-year anniversary. It was a WTF moment, if I have ever had one. Who and why had someone booked a hotel five months in advance for Marcus and Annie, not Marcus and Fiona? Upset, I called Marcus. But his explanation was ridiculous. His mother booked a romantic trip for our upcoming ten-year anniversary? I didn't believe it. All Sheryl had shown me for months was contempt. When I asked who Annie was, she said it was a mistake; the hotel had mistaken "Fiona" for "Annie." Yeah, right. My name has been butchered, but never have I been called Annie. For the first time in weeks, Marcus returned to our condo to take the letter from me. I just couldn't wrap my head around this whole situation, so yet again, I unwittingly buried my head back in the sand.

Can you believe that after my doctors found out about our separation, they informed me that divorce is far more likely when the wife has cancer? God, seriously, let's call a spade a spade; the fact that between 21 to almost 25 percent of husbands ditches their wives after cancer diagnoses is *unthinkable*! I don't understand the rationale; men are soldiers who traditionally wouldn't dream of deserting their fellow soldiers on the battlefield. Why does leaving even enter a man's mind when his wife is waging war on cancer? Some experts say men struggle with the fight-or-flight response to the perceived attack or threat to their survival. It weighs heavily on my heart that so many sick women aren't shown loyalty or devotion by their mates.

Incredibly, husbands only risk a 3 percent chance that their wives will divorce them when they are seriously ill.

What's the excuse for this behavior? Men aren't designed to be caregivers; it's the women who are the nurturers in a relationship. Doesn't this constitute a one-way street? Wouldn't it make sense then that all future grooms leave out the words "in sickness and in health?" Forgive me for spouting off about the dirty little secret that, for housewives, cancer spells D-I-V-O-R-C-E. Possibly cancer treatment should include marriage counseling, since one-quarter of husbands bail. Okay. End of rant. Marcus hurt me and hurt shouldn't pile up like this inside of someone. You should have time to breathe; time to scream it out until you can't scream any longer.

Then, without any notice, Marcus left on another trip, this time a four-week vacation to New York, supposedly to visit his dad. I learned later he spent very little time with his father. By this point, my parents were begging me to move in with them. Sheryl wanted me out of her condo—she lied and said she was renting it to someone else. I tried to be independent, but neuropathy, a nerve disorder had set in. After Marcus left, I drove to the grocery store to buy food for the kids but my arms went completely numb. The bagger at the grocery store started to cry, feeling sorry for me since I couldn't pick the food up out of the basket. She said I was the first person she actually wanted to drive home to make sure I got home safely. Standing there, I was so appreciative for the kindness of a stranger. It was one of those rare moments. You know, when you feel an unexpected human connection. Literally, her concern filled my heart and soul with pure joy.

Pushing forward, I found that my second round of chemo was much harder; I suffered from body aches, memory loss, loss of appetite, and depression. Complications from chemotherapy included the need for blood transfusions, IV fluids for dehydration, and extended hospital stays. Still, I found it impossible to resist the urge to call or text Marcus. It was hard to realize our relationship was over, and I couldn't find the strength to take care of myself and the children. How could I make it without him? I loved him and believed he was my best friend, my soul mate.

During this time, Nieve called Sheryl one afternoon. She was hungry, and she wanted to let her know I was extremely ill on the bathroom floor. For weeks, I vomited many times during the day, unable to eat or drink, without the strength to make it back to bed. There I was, lying on the bathroom floor, covered in vomit, when my mother-in-law placed a sandwich on a plate in front of me. After her lunch with Nieve, she took her swimming at the community pool without a hint of guilt. Imagine how worthless I felt, not even worthy of a helping hand into bed.

Inevitably, I gave in to the idea that I needed assistance. Reaching for help, I put out an all call on Facebook for anyone able to help move the entire contents of our home into storage. So many friends and family showed up and offered their services; of course, Sheryl and Marcus were absent. Surprisingly, Penny showed up at the end of the move, looking very much strung out, in an itty-bitty white tank top. She was distracting the men. They couldn't stop focusing on her breasts as she talked incessantly. Then, there was that moment when all hell broke loose. My father lost it when Sheryl arrived on the scene to take the condominium association's luggage trolley.

Sheryl began yelling as she threw Nieve's belongings off the trolley. That was the last straw. Irate, my dad confronted her. In his Irish accent, he said, "I have a good mind to throw you off that balcony." Mind you, we were on the sixth floor. Yes, I am my father's daughter, so much like him, except when it came to standing up for me. My father stood his ground as Sheryl defended the actions of her youngest son.

The only one not defending himself was Marcus. Scared, I was fighting for my life, losing my battle to save my marriage, and living a nightmare beyond my wildest dreams. There I stood, unable to roar. All I could hear, was a quiet little voice deep inside of me say 'It's going to be okay…We will try again tomorrow.'" Even though I felt weak and weary, I had to encourage myself to find the strength to carry on with my life.

It takes strength to be firm, and it takes courage to be gentle.

It takes strength to conquer, and it takes courage to surrender.

It takes strength to be certain, and it takes courage to have doubt.

It takes strength to fit in, and it takes courage to stand out

It takes strength to feel a friend's pain, and it takes courage to feel your own pain.

It takes strength to endure abuse, and it takes courage to stop it.

It takes strength to stand alone, and it takes courage to lean on another.

It takes strength to love, and it takes courage to be loved.

It takes strength to survive, and it takes courage to live.

—Unknown

Of course, I relinquished the lease to my mother-in-law who, instead of renting it, had the condo freshly painted for the return of her prodigal son. Ironically, the parable of the lost son is the story of a parent forgiving a sinful son. Marcus was definitely a wayward son who lacked morals, who after squandering his time returned home, to his mother's delight. It was hard to remind myself that even if I fell down yesterday and the day before that, it was still possible to stand tall today. Heavyhearted, I knew the emotional pain was overshadowing my will to survive.

Once Marcus confirmed that the bankruptcy had been officially discharged, he wanted his freedom. I wondered why the bankruptcy was so important. What really made me sick to my stomach was the fact my beloved husband left us poverty-stricken. The kids and I were destitute, relying on my family for food and shelter. Truly, I wept for forty days and forty nights after I had been served with the divorce paperwork.

It is difficult to put feelings into words, to express the way I felt during the days, months, and even years after Marcus abandoned me. Certain songs capture those difficult moments. For me, the song "Break Even" epitomized my troubles. *"I'm still alive, but I'm barely breathing, just prayin' to a God that I don't believe in, 'cause I got time, while he got freedom, 'cause when a heart breaks, no, it don't break even."* It is sad but true. When a relationship ends; one person inherently hurts more than the other.

For sure, I still believed in God, but I was lost and insecure, and I blamed God for taking Marcus. Yes, God answered my prayers to save my life, and I did say he could take anything, but I didn't mean take Marcus! My breakup anthem states, *"They say bad things happen for a reason, but no wise words gonna stop the bleeding, 'cause he's moved on, while I'm still grieving"* (The Script). Loving someone who doesn't love you back is an impossible situation. Really, there are no winners in the game of love. Plus I hadn't realized the fact, that loving Marcus meant I was playing with fire, certain to get burned.

During the months of July and August 2010, I spent almost six weeks in the hospital. My weight had plummeted to 108 pounds. I wanted to believe Marcus separated from his ailing wife in order to minimize the pain he'd suffer if I didn't survive. But his actions spoke otherwise; he removed my boys from our family health insurance and took my name off as beneficiary of his life insurance policy. He refused to buy school supplies and uniforms for Connor, since he was no longer his child. Yes, he had left me penniless. Marcus took all the real estate listings, sales, and commissions.

During one of my extended hospitalizations, Marcus unexpectedly showed up at my door. I am not going to lie; it was a pleasant surprise. But he didn't come to hold my hand. He came to grab my breast and whisper in my ear, "You owe me anal sex, and soon you're going to bend over and take it." It was not the sweet nothings or endearing words that would have made me feel safe, comfortable, and—God forbid—loved. Why couldn't he have spoken softly and lovingly to me or tried to hold me close? Marcus had no compassion toward me, in sickness or in health.

The truth can be very hard to hear, especially when you continue to live in denial. It was always easier to listen to Marcus's lies, but at some point I would have to face a situation straight on. Nicole was my son Ryan's girlfriend at the time; she kindly visited me during my numerous hospital stays. During one of her visits, I learned that Penny was Marcus's new play toy. This woman had helped move me out, only to move her furniture in. She claimed to only be decorating his home, but it didn't take long before my old neighbors reported seeing them frolicking and kissing poolside.

Finally, when I had an opportunity to regain normalcy by picking up my kids from school, Marcus's indiscretion was thrown in my face. Penny had her daughter put

Marcus's shorts into Nieve's school backpack. These two little girls were only third graders, yet this insecure woman wanted me to know my husband was now with her. I called her to ask her not to include the children in adult matters, but she began to ramble about how Marcus was back on cocaine again. Of course, knowing that my husband was in the arms and bed of another woman destroyed me.

A real estate writer for our local paper featured my struggles in an article titled "Well-Known Broker Battles for Life." The fact that my husband and business partner filed for divorce during my punishing chemo treatments sent a wave of shock throughout our community. That article was supposed to be a warning to others not to self-diagnose. But the paper dug up our wedding announcement photo and added it to the article. Marcus was irate that his Mr. Wonderful mask had been removed in public. Rage set in as he began to mourn his predicament, the loss of his so-called reputation. But in my opinion, one's reputation is based on one's character. And one of the most important ways to strengthen your character is to show empathy to others, especially those whom you call family.

Marcus became fixated on inflicting as much pain as possible on me. I am forever grateful that my friend and hair stylist cohosted a benefit with my sister and sister-in-law to raise money for my situation. Just prior to the fund-raiser, scheduled for the end of September 2010, Marcus took me to court to stop the cancer benefit. There was no level to which my husband, soon-to-be ex, wouldn't stoop in order to ensure my demise. Fortunately, the judge threw out the case, dismissing his claims that the hosts of the event were auctioning his belongings at the benefit. Literally, he was laughed right out of the district courthouse.

Through phone calls and texts, there were plenty of opportunities for Marcus to enjoy his cruelties. When we exchanged our daughter for visitation, he would torment me, and all the while a smile played over his lips. He truly felt entitled to bend me to his wishes in order to get revenge. All of my emotional pain was a form of entertainment to Marcus. Gleefully smug, he shed his responsibilities to his family. It's more than hurtful; it's excruciatingly painful to know you will never remember all of the things that I will never forget

Chapter 11:

LEGALIZE POT? WHY NOT?

"Some of my finest hours have been spent on my back veranda, smoking hemp and observing as far as my eye can see."
—Thomas Jefferson

Hey, if current and past presidents, used weed, why can't any American do it legally today? I know, I'm just an ordinary housewife but that doesn't change my belief that pot should be legalized, at least for medicinal purposes. It may sound odd, my views on legalizing weed, considering that addiction has definitely negatively affected my family. But did you know that the overall addiction potential for cannabis is less than cigarettes, caffeine, alcohol, cocaine, or heroin? Trust me, the research supports this. You've got a better chance of becoming addicted to a daily cup of Starbucks than to pot. Hell yes, I'm right there with 'em—if I don't get my caffeine fix daily, I'll end up with a horrendous headache.

I do believe my first experience with pot was during my junior year in high school. I can vividly remember taking a hit or two, as the tips of my fingers got a little burned from holding the end of that rolled joint. Clearly, getting high on marijuana made me feel like a rebel, but that didn't take much, since I was raised in a strict Catholic household. Oh yeah, smoking weed was like checking out of reality, temporarily, of course.

As the years passed, I morphed into not only a Stepford wife but also an über-mom, maybe even a superüber-mom. "What the heck is an über-mom?" Well, let's see…My children were the first to have the newest and best clothes and accessories from head to toe, like having Crocs, or even Heelys. Since three years of age, my little girl participated in ballet, and my sons were shuttled to and from soccer, football, and hockey. I volunteered at their private schools, chaperoned for field trips, and was on a first-name basis with the school principal. Year after year, I planned and held huge birthday parties for my children, and each time, I tried to outdo the previous one.

Was I insane? Possibly, but that's another story. Between scheduling my daughter's ever-so-popular play dates and running a real estate mini-empire I discovered my sixteen-year old son smoking weed with a few of his friends. I became irate. Isn't it funny how I forgot all about that teenage girl who also tried pot—me? Blame it on my über-mom persona taking over and prioritizing searching for an appropriate consequence for my son's offense. Really I'm not even sure why I felt our upper-middle-class family should keep up appearances? Blame it on the supermom persona inside of me but at that moment I forced Ryan to 'carry the torch.' So like any other teen, he continued to smoke, all the while keeping it on the down low.

And for a while all was calm, until of course it wasn't. Hell broke loose on Ryan's high-school graduation day. Foolishly, he decided to smoke in public—lakeside in our gated community. Ryan got caught, arrested, and released. Yes, it would be reasonable to accept that my son used cannabis to escape his hellish reality within our household. Who could blame him for wanting to escape Marcus's tyranny? But once I discovered my eldest son's arrest, I became upset, punished Ryan, and reminded him I would never tolerate the use of marijuana.

Now, let's fast forward a few more years. To the time when I am being handed a prescription for both Dronabinol and Nabilon (drugs derived from marijuana) in order to help me with the chemotherapy-related nausea and vomiting. Remember, my weight had plummeted to 108 pounds—too low for my five-foot-ten-inch body. I was unable to put on weight and had hit a point where I myself felt I was too skinny. Finally, I had to be admitted to a local hospital in order to be force-fed through an IV at a cost of a grand per day to my health insurance carrier. After two three-week stays in the cancer ward, I was released, only to start losing weight again.

But fortunately, a member of my oncology team knew exactly what to do about my drastic weight loss. I was urged to get my hands on the real deal—marijuana. As soon as possible. And if I couldn't find help, they implied that help would be sent my way. I cracked a smile, the first in a long time. Instantly, I knew just the person I could ask to help me find a bit of pot. Although, I don't want to mislead you, I was extremely conflicted about asking my child to aid in supplying me with an illegal substance. Think about it, it's not like I didn't spend years yelling about how pot was bad and bad for you. Judge me if you will, and you will. All I can say is that my body was starving itself, because the cancer cells needed more food, more energy.

Not only was I rail thin, but I was weak, constantly sick, and no good to anyone, let alone my children. Many people asked how they could help me get through my cancer treatment, but the sad truth was there really wasn't much they could do. Ryan was twenty years old when I told him what my medical team had suggested. How I wish you could have seen my son's face. Honestly, it lit up like a Christmas tree. He said that as his mother, I had always given to him without question, and now he could finally return the favor.

Physically, my body had hit rock bottom; it was as if I was at the threshold of death, maybe because I was at that point. Still, somewhere deep inside of me I knew my mission in life wasn't yet complete. I was at a crossroads. I needed to make a change or do something different. My survival depended on it. But taking an uncharted path meant I needed to peel away layers of negative thinking, even with regard to using marijuana.

With one phone call from my elder son, his supplier delivered the best weed he offered, on the house. And as soon as I took a few hits, I actually began to feel better— less nauseated, although I have to admit, smoking reefer made me feel a bit spacey. But then, all of a sudden it hit, this amazing moment that seemed to last for hours. I felt as if I was one with the couch—the couch that I was sitting on. Yes, I know this all may sound a little funny, but believe me when I tell you that my whole body felt utterly relaxed. I was in awe, amazed at how quickly so much tension and strain left my sickly body. The feeling I felt at that moment was kind of like those first few moments after you get into a warm bath. Even still, that example doesn't fully describe the euphoria I had just experienced.

Had weed gotten more potent? Or was it just a better quality than I had ever tried? Once the nausea and vomiting stopped, my appetite returned full force in the form of the marijuana munchies. And let me tell you the blessings of pot didn't just stop there. I began to feel an improved sense of well-being, and I was less anxious overall. In my experience, pot made me feel better, much better! Thank the Lord, I could finally get some sleep, and on a full belly, to boot. Pot was definitely a gift from God. But that's not to say I didn't feel like one hell of a hypocrite after years of vilifying cannabis.

Really and truly, it was difficult to reconcile my past and present beliefs on weed, especially when it came to parenting. Of course, I hid my pot use from both Connor and Niove. But finally I am not afraid to admit it—using pot saved my life! Wow, it feels really refreshing to finally stand up and not be afraid to show who I really am, and what I believe in. You get it, right—the freedom to let your beliefs hang out for all to see. I've felt firsthand the beneficial effects of marijuana. And the thought of so many cancer patients needlessly suffering in pain, while research proves marijuana can improve the quality of their lives, just kills me.

During my second round of chemotherapy, I was told about preclinical studies done that show that use of cannabis may inhibit tumor growth by bringing about cell death, choking cell growth, and hampering the development of blood vessels that are needed by tumors to flourish. Sure I'd love to see cannabis become part of the standard therapy for patients suffering with chemotherapy-related nausea and vomiting. And for that matter, why shouldn't our doctors have the freedom to recommend the treatment they deem appropriate for their patients?

Honestly, I have the attitude of gratitude for all the doctors, nurses, and medical staff that saved my life. And how can I not be grateful, now that I find myself in the position to help others. I needed to be thankful for what I had. For when I concentrated on what I didn't have, I was unable to appreciate all of the gifts and lessons given to me. So when I focus on today, I am incredibly thankful for all of those memories, good or bad, with regard to my battle with cancer. I am so grateful to those doctors and nurses who spoke out, encouraging me to use weed regardless of its legality. Then, there is the fact that my relationship with my oldest son became stronger, because he was able to come to my rescue.

Maybe I will be the toke of the town, by coming out in support of legalizing pot, but frankly, my dear, I don't give a damn. All I know is marijuana became my ally in my fight to regain my life. So what if I looked like Barbie, and smoked like Marley? Why not use nature's pot of gold? You really can't judge, unless you've been in my shoes. Remember, as the use of medical marijuana spreads across the United States, lives are being saved. Just think of pot as another weapon to aid in the fight against cancer. Why let another person suffer when we have the means to control some of the side effects of chemotherapy? What if your loved one were ill with cancer? What would you want for them?

Chapter 12:

NUMBER ONE PRIEST, NOW RELEASED

"It's toughest to forgive ourselves. So it's probably best to start with other people. It's almost like peeling an onion. Layer by layer, forgiving others, you really do get to the point where you can forgive yourself."
—Patty Duke

I guess, to be completely honest, the first time I really felt rejected by the Catholic Church was in Rome when I tried to go to confession. Being rejected caused me to pause, but instead of questioning my religion, I blindly did what the priest asked of me. I returned to Florida in pursuit of an annulment. I mean, according to the church, *"that which God has joined together, no human being must separate"* (Matthew 19:6). Yes, Garrett and I had a civil divorce, but that wasn't enough, I wanted our marriage to be null and void in the eyes of God. At least an annulment wouldn't affect the legitimacy of our kids; Ryan was already born out of wedlock.

If the truth be told, a civil divorce meant we were once married, but an annulment would declare we were never truly married at all. Sure at first, I wanted an annulment so that I could marry Marcus in front of God. But seriously after I got it, I really didn't want to bring God into our marital mess. I do realize that I was partly to blame; I did ignore Marcus's faults, or at least didn't take enough time to let them surface. And hell to the yes, both of my marriages were rough roads traveled, fraught with ups and downs. Why until my illness, I was too afraid to question my religion. You know, the fact we are all born into it versus our beliefs.

There were times when I felt I couldn't express my own individuality in the Catholic Church. Was I just a part of the controlled masses, brainwashed to believe what I had been told? I have seen religion be the drug of choice for others—an unhealthy addiction when the commitment crosses the line to dependence. Since childhood, most Sundays I would avoid church, tired of sitting, standing, and kneeling at mass. Isn't blind faith in religion as bad as blind faith in science? Sure, my search for truth started when I began using my ability to reason, to learn but it took decades for me to question my life and the way I chose to live it.

Knowing myself, really knowing myself, meant I had to look at how I was raised and why I chose Garrett and for that matter, Marcus. Every hospitalization, no matter how lonely I was, was a revelation for me. The sad truth was, 99.9 percent of the time, I worried about my husband, instead of my health. Instead of looking for answers, I really needed to be asking the right questions. Of course, back then my mind was clouded. There was just no way I could flip my thoughts around. I felt defeated, not good enough. Instead of waking up, feeling privileged to be alive, I kept asking, why me? Instead of asking why *not* me?

I needed to judge only my level of responsibility in the marriage. In fact, I needed to do that for both marriages. Really I needed to do was be my own best friend or at least a better friend to myself.

Pausing for a moment to let those words sink in made a huge difference in my life. At first it felt awkward, but over time I began to back myself up instead of put myself down. Then in October 2010, I was rushed to the emergency room with acute abdominal pain. Over and over, a suction tube was forced down my nose, in order to aid with my intestinal obstruction. My surgeon, Dr. Dyke, wanted to wait and see if there was any way my body could clear the bowel obstruction in its own time.

Can you believe that—right then and there, in the midst of another medical complication—Marcus showed up? Why wouldn't he want to take center stage and profess his undying love toward me? Yet again, he found another opportunity to manipulate his image. Gaining superficial attention was so important to him. And by allowing him to stay, I made the decision to embark yet again on an orgy of self-destruction. Marcus visited each day and night, complaining of how bored he was without me. His words truly felt hollow. Funny thing is when I was forced to stand alone, it was then, and only then that I realized what I was really made of. Amazingly, I found a wealth of inner reserves and strength I didn't know existed.

Daily, my husband projected his bad character onto me, intimidating me with our impending divorce if I didn't do as I was told. It didn't matter that I was skeletal thin or being force-fed; Marcus wanted to control and punish me for his pain. Every evening he debased me sexually. Marcus insisted I give him hand jobs as he tormented my body; I was too weak to fight back. With every ounce of his being he loathed me, maybe he feared me, too—he was nothing short of a misogynist. I always refused, but he kept insisting he wanted anal sex. What the hell was he thinking, I couldn't even have a bowel movement, and he knew it! Why did he keep objectifying me? Moreover, why had I again become a submissive, adoring, and self-sacrificing wife?

I was utterly confused. My submission bred Marcus's superiority. Family and friends were baffled by the giant shadow cast by Marcus. Everyone in Marcus's presence could feel the mayhem he caused; it was that simple. Sure, I hated that I was clingy, uncertain, and frightened. Even the hospital staff witnessed the long chain of humiliations and subjugation. He was a force to be reckoned with; not many were able to fight his tyranny. Marcus controlled all my visitors; his evil was constantly trying to masquerade as good.

Dr. Dyke finally decided surgery was required to treat my blockage. Thank God, she also agreed to the ileostomy reversal.

Father Fagan held a prayer service during my surgery, which became a bone of contention for my husband. When I awoke from my surgery, I was inundated with complaints, because no one wanted to pray with him. Marcus had no concern for my health; to him, nothing existed except himself. How dare he be ignored? All who really knew Marcus had long since labeled him a pathological liar with no empathy for his wife and kids. Yes, my friends and family refused to be a part of his immoral behavior. By this point, they all but regarded him as subhuman. My spouse couldn't believe it. He had lost control. He was no longer able to manipulate loved ones, and literally he began losing his mind.

Looking back, maybe it wasn't that surprising that he tried to reassert his control by forging a fictitious reconciliation with me. It's not like there was any give and take going on. And there I was again, compromising my very soul in order to spend time with this man. Why couldn't I move forward without him? Still, I couldn't see clearly, even when a nurse told me my husband was the first man she had ever witnessed who truly wanted his wife dead.

Finally, Halloween rolled around, and he invited me to our old condo to be his plaything. I wore a hat and rode the service elevator, so his mother wouldn't find out we were back together again.

Surreptitiously, Marcus used my vulnerability and need for human affection in order to receive as much sexual pleasure as possible. It was then and there, that he demanded a blow job. But call it karma if you will, or that no one has the right to demand sex, but during the act, I vomited all over his penis. Maybe it was the chemo that day, or the fact that I was still extremely ill, but needless to say, my husband was furious! Still to this day, I can't clear my mind of that image. Honestly, it looked a little like dick chutney down there.

During those days, Marcus put me to work in his open houses, promising security, but he was really just putting on a show for his clients. I was kept on the edge of sanity while he used me as a sex object. Having sex in his sellers' homes gave my husband a huge adrenaline rush. He felt powerful, so whenever the mood struck him, he would call, use, and dispose of me. For Marcus, it just didn't matter where, when, or why, it was that all sexual activity was under his control. By Thanksgiving, I was forced to see that I had been played. This guy I loved kept all commissions hidden. He lied. All of his tactics had killed my spirit and trampled my soul. I was caught off guard when Marcus decided to call it quits again, for the second time.

How had Barbie become the epitome of sub-missiveness, walking on eggshells in front of Donnie? Anger set in as I reacted to Marcus's lies and abuse.

My life definitely had not measured up to my childhood expectations. It didn't matter that I had apologized a million times. Once Marcus detached, he was gone. Being abandoned twice in less than six months had left me in pieces. There wasn't anything I wouldn't have done to keep our marriage together. Well, that's not exactly true—I never caved in and gave Marcus anal sex.

Within a few weeks of second separation, I happened to speak with Marcus's old girlfriend, Jillian. For almost thirteen years, I had been led to believe that I was abnormal, since his past girlfriend loved anal intercourse. But Jillian told a different story. Can you believe she had been sleeping when Marcus inserted his penis in her anus for his sexual pleasure? In my humble opinion, that sounds like anal rape to me, not a special moment shared by two consenting adults. How sad that she was another victim of Marcus's abusive behavior. Her experience had left her feeling fragile and fearful, not allowing her to perform that act with her current husband. After this conversation, I knew Marcus had left a trail of many victims. Anyone was ripe for raping—physically, emotionally, or spiritually.

By the time Christmas arrived, I was contemplating suicide, raw from our breakup. And yet, I was willing to do anything to have Marcus back in my life. Still of course, my reality was distorted. I was obsessed with saving my horrible marriage.

It was then that Father Fagan announced his intention to move back to Africa for missionary work. He felt God's calling and believed he would best serve God in helping the poor. Still ill, I wanted to make the time to say good-bye. Besides, I needed to discuss some spiritual matters.

Father Fagan pushed for our meeting to be in the privacy of his home, but I wanted a quick meet and greet in public. I feared he wanted me to list his home for sale or put it up for rent, neither of which I was interested in doing. Perhaps it was the fact that we had shared a few awkward phone calls around this time. On one of those calls, he inquired about how my romantic life was developing. At the time, I was planning a trip to Ireland, hoping maybe I'd meet someone there. To my utter surprise, Father Fagan asked if he flew to Ireland, would I consider dating him. Was he joking? "You're a priest,"

I said. He laughed and said, "I know, I know." I rushed off the phone, feeling incredibly awkward.

In actual fact, I should have listened to my instincts and not agreed to meet Father Fagan—at Perkins, of all places. From the moment I arrived, Father Fagan kept complimenting my appearance, so much so that I quickly became very uncomfortable. He said that there was nothing wrong with him admiring my physical beauty. I responded, "I thought your job was to be concerned with my spiritual side." He smiled devilishly as he continued to stare through me. Dear God, this meeting had become unnerving. I just wanted to hurry this up and leave. I told him I couldn't represent him as his broker, but I would gladly refer another agent. But he wasn't interested in discussing his home, not that day.

I had to go. My stomach was hurting, stress induced, of course. Finally, we were saying good-bye, and Father Fagan insisted on walking me to my car. But once there, he further insisted on sitting inside my car to discuss one more issue. He seemed sincere but pushy. I told him to make it quick, because I had some family obligations. Once inside my car, he began telling me how he had pictured saying good-bye to me. He wanted a good-bye kiss, which I thought meant a kiss on the cheek. Instead he forcefully grabbed my face and pulled me in for a full-blown romantic kiss. Was he out of his fucking mind? Gross, gross, gross!

I struggled to push him off me. This old man—or should I say dirty old man—was a priest, for God's sake. And not just any priest, our family priest, who married me to Garrett and baptized most of the children within our family. Gees, he really was a big part of our family. Irritated and in shock, I ordered him out of my car. As he exited, he grabbed the door and asked me if this could be our little secret. Fear flooded his face. Did I mention this priest was in his eighties? Talk about a man of the cloth taking advantage of a sick woman in a vulnerable position. Honestly, I felt like I needed a shower. Something dirty had touched me, both physically and spiritually.

Definitely, he abused his power and our friendship, and he made me question my religion even more. Thank goodness, I never agreed to meet him in the privacy of his own home. I can only imagine what he would have tried. Friends and family spoke with Father Fagan's superiors. We later learned, he was transferred up north for psychological testing, saving who knows how many women in Africa from his overtures. Whether I was aware of it or not, this trauma would linger on for years, making me doubt my religion, my spirituality. I was traumatized and left in a more fragile state than before this meeting. How much more could I endure at the hands of men I trusted? I didn't know if I would ever be able to forgive Father Fagan. But one thing was for sure, my number-one priest, in one unforgettable moment was released.

Chapter 13:

HOW MANY THERAPISTS DID IT TAKE?

"For the love of God, folks, don't try this at home."
—David Letterman

Have you heard the one, how many therapists does it take to change a light bulb? One, but the light bulb has to really want to change. I guess the bottom line is that change is really all about one's desire to change. Yes, it took me years, even decades to really want to change. And no, I am not opposed to working with counselors, therapists, psychologists, social workers, or psychiatrists. I guess my first experience with marriage counseling tainted me. How many therapists do you know who give oral sex to their clients? Not many, right? Who can blame me for being gun-shy from that experience? Was I wrong to expect a counselor to uphold clear, compassionate values?

Khalil Gibran's words make a valid point. *"Out of suffering have emerged the strongest souls: the most massive characters are seared with scars."* Who among us hasn't been a slave to emotional suffering? From the moment Marcus walked out on us, I was thrown off balance, staggering violently as his actions and words rubbed my soul raw.

Ever since my misdiagnosis of terminal cancer, I had been on a combination of antidepressants and antianxiety medications. As each month passed in 2010, I became more severely depressed. These so-called "happy pills" didn't block out any of my pain or eliminate my feelings of worthlessness. Let's be honest, I was just seen as collateral damage, but I was the one who allowed him to reduce me to an object. Once I was broken and damaged, I no longer had value, to him and to myself.

For as long as I can remember, I didn't allow myself to trust my intuition, relying on Marcus's words, not focusing on his actions. I definitely suffered from insecurity and low self-esteem. Everyone can be insecure, but self-assurance starts with accepting uncertainty. Really, why in hell did I rescue my partners? Admittedly, I forfeited all my power— and my ability to take care of myself—in order to please someone else. Deep down I wanted to believe that one day they would reciprocate and be there when I needed them most.

After the physical abuse occurred with Garrett, I visited a center for women in abusive relationships. Yet I didn't have the discipline to let go of our marriage. Really, I just hadn't learned my lessons well enough. I needed more time to learn I couldn't love an abusive personality into treating me well. Constantly, I was swimming in my thoughts and feelings of inadequacy, fearful that Garrett would leave me. There was a part of me that was afraid of looking this situation square on and accepting the fact that our relationship was not a loving one. Acceptance of what had happened was the first step toward overcoming the effects of little to no self love.

Right after, I discovered Marcus's drug addiction, I reached out to Nancy Shore, a specialist in behavioral and emotional health for families. I knew my entire family needed to address Marcus's substance abuse. It had affected each of us and our relationships. Both boys struggled with the fact that their father and stepfather abused cocaine. Truly, I needed professional help to address all their questions. There was no guarantee that our children might avoid inheriting the disease of alcoholism or of drug addiction. And at that time, Marcus was so self-absorbed that he was unable to see how much he had harmed the children.

Now I realize I shouldn't have listened to my husband when he begged to return home after rehab. He needed to show me through his actions that he wanted to change. Our sessions with Nancy became nothing but a waste of my husband's time, a humiliating chore in order to regain his life and social status. Marcus wanted his life back, but he didn't want to work at staying clean and sober. He called Nancy a "Jew bitch" as a way of dumping his shame onto her. Yet I was the one who returned for individual therapy with Ms. Shore after Marcus blindsided me with his abrupt departure.

Between losing my house, cars, commercial building, and business, not to mention bankruptcy, looming divorce, and cancer, I desperately needed help. I was overwhelmed by this earth-shattering series of events. The weird thing is that Marcus decided to attend a couple of my therapy sessions during this time. To him, therapy was a competitive sport; obviously he still held Nancy in contempt, yet he wanted to play mind games with her. It was all about the drama. It's not as if he wanted to reunite with me. It was at this time that Ms. Shore discovered both of our personality disorders. By adolescence, each of us had deeply ingrained and maladaptive patterns of behavior.

Our personalities caused us to have long-term difficulties in relationships. I crossed paths with Marcus because I was a love addict, suffering from a codependent personality disorder. This meant I was living through or for another person. Here is the real kicker: honestly, up until that moment I didn't realize that my husband was a full-blown narcissist. Narcissus was a character in Greek mythology that fell in love with his own reflection in a pool of water. So isn't narcissism when a person is in love with his or her own reflection in a mirror? My spouse's grandiose sense of self-importance, requirement for excessive admiration, lack of empathy, and fantasies of unlimited success and ideal love had added up to one hell of a serious disorder.

I knew Marcus's arrogance, envy, and exploitative and haughty behavior were inherently dysfunctional. But as a codependent, I was the natural magnet for narcissistic individuals, including Garrett, Marcus, and even Father Fagan. Under the influence of an alcoholic parent, I grew up codependent. And obviously a string of dysfunctional relationships formed afterward. My identity evolved as a pleaser, fixer, and compulsive giver. I was stuck in a negative loop, filled with poor boundaries and low self-esteem. I cared too much about others. Fortunately, therapy became a time to redirect my love addiction toward myself.

Within about six weeks of our divorce, Marcus had moved in with Annie. Throughout my illness, my second ex-husband went out of his way to ensure I didn't know about his infidelities. If only he had admitted to cheating, I might have reacted accordingly. Annie was surely put on a pedestal and told how much happier he was with her—she somehow had saved him from my abuse. He wore a new mask, ever so innocent, and he pointed to my desperate texts and messages in order to evoke her sympathy. Was I still to believe that the reservation made by my ex-mother-in-law for my anniversary wasn't made for this Annie?

Aren't we all a little crazy at some point during our lives? Trust me; you don't go crazy all at once. It takes a lot to question your own sanity. But sometimes, it really is the correct and appropriate response to your reality to go insane, if only for a second or two.

Sadly, I based my self-worth on my ability to give, give, and give some more. In other words, I defined myself by the men in my life and lived solely to please them. Of course, it's not healthy to have one's self-esteem dependent upon others. It was going to take a lot of therapy to heal, since I had been living in a wasteland of self-worth for over two decades. What I had to learn was to love myself and make myself comfortable. Was it unfortunate that I partnered with my ex-husbands? I think not. Those marriages were lessons. I needed to learn how to confront my own issues.

Exhaustion set in after two failed relationships. What would I do with my need to be wanted? Honestly, I liked being a giver; I took a lot of pride in my willingness to go above and beyond to make the people I love happy. As one of six children, I definitely needed my parents to tell me that I did a good job before I could feel good about my accomplishments. Pleasing was a way of escaping, dealing with my own emotions. It took me forty years to grasp the concept that I was only responsible for what I did or said. To hell with everyone's reactions.

I put my relationships above myself; I refused to put my oxygen mask on first. Truthfully, I had no concept of how to care for myself. Isn't there great madness in love? Why is that? Why do we always make excuses for acting crazy in love, or when love betrays us? Something deep down and horrible inside of us, feels lethal, on the verge of frenzy when love goes wrong. Truly, our mask of sanity begins to slip without reason. It's crazy when you think about it. These words perfectly describe how I felt on the day I met Marcus and his new lover. We were having issues regarding our daughter's visitation schedule.

All I can say is that I was drawn into the lion's den, a situation in which I surely would have to deal with an angry person or two. In my defense, I felt a very strong magnetic pull drawing me toward that moment. I wanted my child back; too many games were being played, and I needed to take a stand. No, really I wasn't thinking clearly. I didn't fully understand what I was getting myself into. Again, I should have remembered that Marcus was a narcissist and a sociopath. But I had let the psychobabble run in and out of mind, heart, and soul. I hadn't researched, studied, or even accepted the severity of his personality disorders.

Once I arrived on his doorstep, standing next to a police officer, I knew I was unprepared for what I was about to see. Marcus was confronted with our visitation paperwork, but the officer was unable to physically return our child to me. It was a civil matter for the courts. Within seconds, I was being intimidated in a nightmarish fashion. Then a very short, extremely muscular woman appeared in the doorway. In a mannish voice, she shouted, "We have more money than you, and we will be taking your daughter away from you!" Not surprising was the way Marcus was smiling, shirtless, enjoying the drama.

Yes, his lover tried to humiliate me. She called her sister, Kelsey, a local news reporter, and screamed, "Fiona is here to take Nieve! Can you come to my house with a news camera crew?" At least Nieve was not witnessing any of this crap. Later I learned the best approach with a narcissist is to have absolutely no contact. I knew he was easily provoked; his rage had already turned physical. Just weeks before, he had pushed me down a flight of stairs at an open house he was hosting. It has been three years since this incident, and I have never met or laid eyes on Annie again. She was the millionaire of my ex-husband's dreams. But when she told me they would take my daughter away from me, I just couldn't deal with my reality anymore.

Meeting her, seeing him, hit me with such magnitude that I reeled, completely thrown off balance—raw. The encounter was so painful, I returned home and overdosed on every prescription pain medication I had in my medicine cabinet. Yet again, I wasn't thinking clearly. I just didn't want to feel—you know, feel the emotional pain of being.

After my suicide attempt, the one question nobody asked was why. Everyone already knew I was unable to cope with all that had happened in my personal life. After my stomach was pumped, I was "Baker Acted" into a psych ward. Now, of course, I feel the guilt of putting my children through all of that. I was diagnosed with situational depression, which is also known as reactive depression.

Surprisingly, my doctor felt I was reacting normally to the recent events in my life. Still, in the aftermath of all that had happened, I had to deal with continued depression, tearfulness, and feelings of hopelessness. Finally, I hit my low—that point in life where something's got to give. It took a trip to the cuckoo house to want to change—pick myself up, dust myself off, and start over. Yes, there was a slight glimmer of hope. Yes, I may have been surrounded by a few disturbed people there, but honestly, I met some of the sanest human beings I have ever met. I cried tears of joy when I walked out of that psych ward; it felt like the sun broke through storm clouds that had been lingering over my head.

It was time to start to build myself up physically, mentally, and spiritually. I remember doing a painting in art therapy of the kids and me as flowers in a garden, with my ex as the weed trying to choke the life out of us. No longer would I allow anyone to hurt those flowers. Finally, I was grateful to be free and alive. For no matter how despairingly, acutely miserable I had been, somehow I have made it through to the other side. Seriously, there is light at the end of the tunnel. To be alive is really a gift, one that I didn't want to take for granted anymore.

Chapter 14:

THE "BIG C" TO ME IS MY CHILDREN

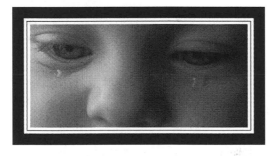

"There is a thin line that separates laughter and pain, comedy and tragedy, humor and hurt."
—Erma Bombeck

All and all, I spent a lot of time trying to heal from my appalling marriage and battle with colon cancer. But no matter how miserable I was—and at times still am—it has been, and still is, hard to face how much emotional pain my kids have suffered through. All that pain came from the hands of all their parents, me included. No doubt, it took me way too long to make progress and heal myself. And at what cost? Well, I'll tell you at what cost—my children became collateral damage, and that's just not acceptable.

Sure, I was struggling with the Big C (cancer), but so were my children and everyone who loved me. Their lives since my cancer diagnosis were anything but simple or easy. Ryan, Connor, and Nieve lost their sense of emotional security as they watched their mother fight her malignancy and inevitable divorce.

You see, the thing is, I spent my whole life doing "normal." You know—doing what is expected of every member of society, especially with regard to parenthood. Since their birth, my children were and still are my whole world. I wanted to make their world perfectly normal. Obviously, as I know now, there is no such thing as an über-mom. But as you well know, I repeatedly tried my best to grab that unattainable title. I was exhausted, running my kids from sports to tutoring, trying to create wonderful memories while hiding their fathers' issues. It took facing the possible end to my life to discover what Whoopi Goldberg already knew: *"Normal is nothing more than a cycle on a washing machine."*

In the last three years, my children and I have moved not once, or twice, but nine times in order to find a safe haven to call home. It was difficult to rip the roof from over my children's heads over and over and over. We all know, a child's home means security and routines, and let's face it; it is just basic parenting 101 that kids thrive on routines. Of course, I dragged myself out of my last hospital bed to try to reenter my old career, but it was fruitless. Not only was I still sick, but my ex-husband and business partner, Marcus, sabotaged my career. Since we were a team in the past, we shared the same real estate territory and clients. Much like friends choosing sides after a divorce, our customers chose sides. I guess a lot of my former clientele felt that I was unable to perform my job as well as I had before my cancer diagnosis, and to some degree they were correct.

As I took things day by day, I continued to worry about my children and taking care of their future, all the while struggling with my outstanding medical bills. For the financial impact of treating my cancer had hit my family like a Mack truck. Really, I shouldn't have been trying to return to work, since I was dealing with a barrage of complications from the colon cancer. At the end of almost every day, I cried myself to sleep, wondering why I wasn't lucky enough to have had a partner who could have lovingly supported me and the children through the cancer and recovery. But that's not the type of man I married. At that time, Marcus was too busy hijacking my e-mail account, hacking into my business e-mails, and contacting my prospects.

Even when I tried to hold open houses, he would steal my signage so no one could find my listings. Can you believe it? He even sent phony clients my direction to ask questions about my personal life. Really, what kind of people would do that? Oh and FYI, when your business partner leaves you high and dry while you're ill, you're basically screwed.

What made matters worse was we still worked out of the same office and I was unable to switch due to finances. At one point, I took on a partner, but Wendy was harassed by Marcus to the point where she backed out of our partnership. I couldn't win, and that was the point. Marcus wanted to win by my losing at making any money or any life for my family.

Without any alimony, I had to push forward and work. As I failed to bring in the income we needed, we were continually forced to move, only to move again. The kids and I struggled beyond my wildest dreams. Poverty surrounded and engulfed us. Healthwise, I was grateful to be in remission. But still I struggled with a lot of pain and suffering with severe residual symptoms. I tried to find a life beyond cancer, but I still faced neuropathy, incontinence, fatigue, major changes to my diet, and major joint pain. And chemo had all but destroyed my memory, so I had to learn to live with "chemo brain."

And geez, as if all this wasn't enough, I had to deal with constant watery and explosive diarrhea. I know…I know…*gross*! But I was dealt this hand, and I just had to learn to live with a new normal as my body continued to heal. There was one funny story, though. In 2011, I was pulled over by a cop for speeding after the Fourth of July fireworks show. He approached my window, and I was almost in tears. I told him, "I've just pooped my pants; that's why I'm speeding. I need to get to the nearest bathroom. Sorry, Officer, but I'm recovering from colon cancer." You should have seen his face; I'm not sure who was more embarrassed. He looked me up and down and asked, "Are you telling the truth?" Fortunately for me, I think he smelled something because seconds later he let me go without even a warning.

While I continued to struggle at work, my children began acting out. Ryan's anger at Marcus's cruelty and Garrett's indifference played out in the form of increased partying. Connor started to turn inward, cutting off his friends and family. He struggled to understand the point of attending school when he could end up just like me—a broke college graduate. Not to say he didn't have a point; he did. Again, here comes that idea of "normal" and what is expected of a child, a student, and getting ahead. He graduated middle school only to struggle with high school. "Why should I get a college degree and end up like you?" was one of his favorite comebacks as I fought with him to stay in school. It's not that Connor isn't bright; he's actually very intelligent, and intuitive enough to know I wasn't the best role model for how to end up in life.

I still can't believe that my little boy ended up in and out of four different high schools by his sophomore year. Although Connor and I fought about truancy, I was grateful to God because things could have been a whole lot worse. I know, in my heart of hearts, that Connor, my middle child, was without a doubt the hardest hit emotionally. Twenty-four–seven he was forced to witness the trauma in our household. He doesn't forgive me for the time I focused on mending my horrific marriage. It was then that he started to slip off into a deep depression. I'm not sure if I forgive myself for allowing this to happen to him. I mean, okay, so what if there's no instruction book on how to raise children alone, after you're abandoned, fighting cancer, without any financial security. Why couldn't I have been stronger?

At least now I can thank Jesus for the fact my son decided to get his GED, passed, and enrolled in a local college. So what if his path in school wasn't the so-called norm, at least he's moving toward a brighter future. And he has the admirable goal of one day joining the marines and making a life for himself, one that doesn't include poverty or hunger.

And as for Ryan, he still remembers Marcus yelling at him on our wedding day, "You'd better not ruin my day." And with that memory, he believes in "Marcus's day," that day when all his ex-stepfather's chickens will come home to roost, because there is no way to avoid karma. We all inevitably will face the day when what we have done unto others will be done unto us. Of course, Ryan harbors some pain, angst, and disappointment, but he truly feels the worst is behind us.

Then there's my little girl, Nieve, who was only eight years old at the time of my treatment. She was a front-row witness to Marcus's philandering. Her cross to bear is that she is the biological child of a grossly narcissistic father. She must play her part alone within the walls of her dad's new home. Never being too dramatic, playing the role of the loving daughter, all the while trying to make her dad proud. An impossible task, if you ask me, especially for someone so young.

It is extremely difficult to see the change in Nieve over the past few years. Conforming to Marcus's demands has given way to more than a few angry outbursts. All she really wants is to feel both of her parents' love while being appreciated for just being herself. Is that too much to ask? Seemingly so, since Marcus continues to do whatever it takes, including blame, guilt, emotional neglect, anger, and criticism to bend Nieve to his will.

What of Garrett and his sons? Well, the truth be told, he doesn't play much of a role in the boys' lives. I did return to court after my second divorce in order to enforce child support for at least Connor. The courts awarded me a $30,000+ judgment for over ten years of unpaid child support. But that judgment isn't worth the paper it's written on; I'll be lucky if I get payments from Garrett's social security in a couple of decades. As for visiting their father, Connor went to see his dad for a couple of weeks after Marcus walked out on us. He returned after a week because he was overwhelmed by Garrett's need to justify his addictions.

Connor was an only an eighth grader, too young to be the shoulder for his father to cry on. I had hoped it could be the other way around—Connor being able to lean on his dad. Then, this past summer, Ryan and Connor traveled up north to visit with their paternal grandparents and father, but things took a turn for the worse. Ryan ending up breaking down over Garrett's lack of interest in him and his brother, so both boys returned home early. So now Ryan believes that there's no point trying to work on a nonexistent relationship with his biological father. Connor hasn't weighed in with his opinion yet; he is still trying to recover from all that has happened.

The boys have said that they want to be hands-on fathers when they have kids. Both of my sons faced most of their lives without any real father figure to look up to. Watching my lovely boys turn into young men feeling unloved, even unworthy has always been gut wrenching! They are loved unconditionally by me, their mother. And I am sorry for the pain I have caused them and their sister. It is my goal to replace all that has been taken from them— us—emotionally, physically, and financially. Ryan actually prefers our current life of poverty over a life of financial security with Marcus, but Connor's opinion differs.

As expected with Marcus, Nieve has the best holidays, lovely clothes, a fancy home, everything that will feed her father's ego. And for the most part, Nieve understands the difference between material possessions vs. genuine happiness. I believe she finds happiness in my arms.

It has not been an easy road. At first I was barely alive, broken, limping through a sea of mud, trying to regain any sense of self, all the while wondering, "why couldn't I have protected my children more?'

Now, the 'Big C' in my life always will be my children. After the divorce, Connor, who was just a teenager, actually resented me. There were many moments of hatred and anger directed toward me. He was angry with God for letting such doom and gloom fall upon his family. I was the only parent still standing in front of him, so I had to take on all that pain. He no longer looked at me with love, but with shame, as he turned inward. And I didn't want to address how much

I had hurt him, and the others, by wasting so much time crying over spilled sour milk—Marcus.

It is impossible to describe the scars my children wear upon their hearts and souls. Sadly, their childhood and teenage fun were prematurely cut short as result of the poverty brought on from the divorce and the cancer. And on top of this, now they are prone to addiction, and they may even grow up to be narcissists. Only time will tell if any of my children will develop a false self, using intimidation and aggression to get their way. Scary, right?

But no matter how dark our lives have become, my kids still light up my world. Humor has allowed light to shine through on many dark moments. It's hard to stay mad at someone who makes us laugh. So, needless to say, when I asked Connor a few questions to gauge his feelings about all that has happened, he gave me humor, he gave me light!

Connor said, "It was pure stupidity to get back together with Marcus," and based on that action alone I am the dumbest person he knows. An honest answer, and if my child is anything, he is above all honest. As for my interest in writing, my younger son doesn't see the point, since no one will ever read *Raw* with the exception of a few family members and friends. And since *Raw* isn't going to earn our family a nickel, I'm just wasting time. Lastly, Connor laughed as he told me, "If you ever meet Oprah to discuss your book, I swear, I will personally cut my dick off!"

Strong words from my eighteen-year-old. But trust me; I'll take anger over depression any day. We are making strides, finally! I don't blame Connor for being angry. He lost his house and his father figures; his mom got cancer and then a divorce, and if that wasn't enough, his mother tried to take her own life. We moved, and moved…Really, I am so grateful Connor's kept his sense of humor intact. He constantly makes his brother, sister, and me laugh about the current state of our affairs.

So what if our lives are not perfect? We do have each other. And who out there doesn't have a disastrous dysfunctional family or relationship story? All I can do is continue to learn from my mistakes and guide my children. We are just now starting to live our lives on our own terms. That's not to say there aren't any dark days. There are. I continue have fears about the cancer recurring, and how things could actually still spiral downward.

But what I have done is stopped all my crying. I've stopped trying to be an über-supermom, because that title is just another illusion, or trap. Today, if I see a wannabe über-mom coming my way, trust me, I run the other direction. At first glance—and maybe the second or third glances as well—there appears a woman—a housewife— a mother— who has it all. But I err on the side of caution here, because no mother has it all together, not me, or you, or them!

I try not to focus on the tears that we have all shed but on our current laughter. I'll tell you what, that Mark Twain knew his stuff when he said "What is joy without sorrow? What is success without failure? What is a win without a loss? What is health without illness? You have to experience each if you are to appreciate the other. There is always going to be suffering. It's how you look at your suffering, how you deal with it that will define you."

You bet, we made it through some extremely difficult times, but each trial made us better, not bitter, and that was our lesson learned. Today, for the most part, my children only shed tears of joy.

Chapter 15:

ON THE CHOPPING BLOCK

*"My mouth has been my greatest asset
and my biggest Achilles' heel."*
—Andy Cohen

My whole life, I've been told by others that I am an open book. I guess being an open book just reveals the true nature of my personality, kind of like the car I drive or the sort of TV shows I consume. Yes sir, I've been hooked on so-called reality television programs since I watched the first season of *Real World* on MTV. You bet I'm a fan of watching others air their dirty laundry in public.

But at one point I didn't just want to watch reality TV, I wanted to be a participant. Right after Marcus and I returned from our honeymoon, I actually had our wedding videographer help me create a video so I could try out for *Survivor*. I don't know why, but I got so pumped up with the idea of facing those challenges while competing for like, a million bucks. Although the video showcased me surviving a variety of natural disasters, I didn't receive a call back. As you know, not long after we wed, I became preggers. So, of course, wouldn't you know it that's the moment I received a call from a reality TV show.

Dog Eat Dog was another game show, hosted by Brooke Burns. Someone from the *Survivor* show had passed my video on to the producers of *Dog Eat Dog*, who wanted to see if I had any interest in becoming a contestant for their new program. Who wouldn't want to compete with the opportunity for a paycheck, all the while challenging yourself? But sadly it was not to be, because I was in no condition to compete in any physical competitions; the timing was off. So just like so many other folks, I was left to fantasize about living in that world, the reality TV world.

But truly, I really am just as happy on this side of the television set—in my comfy home, hangin' out in my jammy jams while watching other peeps private lives. I clearly remember gazing into Ozzy Osbourne's personal life. Ozzy really was one of the first big names to open up his home, family, and private life to the public. Actually, Sharon Osbourne, his wife was quoted as saying "He really was the first." Obviously, the public was intrigued since the show was a huge success. I think that show really introduced the category of celebrity reality television.

A few more years passed, and still the itch to be on reality TV hadn't waned. So I applied for *Wife Swap*. It didn't take long before I got a call back. But of course

Marcus was less than enthusiastic and firmly refused to participate. It didn't matter that we as a family had a real shot of being chosen to take part in what I thought would be a mind-blowing challenge. Nonetheless, Marcus couldn't be swayed. He screamed about how I'd be on a vacation while he would just be stuck with some fat slob. So, I dropped the issue. I guess I was just another desperate housewife, on a perfect day, in a perfect neighborhood, in a perfect house, bored, or tortured by my seemingly perfect fake life.

As mad as this may sound, watching reality TV shows like *The Real Housewives of Orange County* (or Atlanta) got me through many long and restless nights during my illness. There were countless hours, days, and sometimes weeks when I was trapped in bed with very little to do. You can relate, right? Just think back to being sick as a child, and all you felt like doing was lying in front of the TV. There were lots of times I couldn't eat or drink, but oh, how I did love watching my favorite shows on Bravo. Thus, the image of me on the back of this book is my homage to the ladies of *The Real Housewives* shows. I mean, I just have to give props to all these housewives, because watching them has definitely been my guilty pleasure. The shows are just so dramatic—the clothes, the parties, the careers (or lack thereof)—truly, it's entertainment at its best.

Since *The Real Housewives of OC* hold oranges, and *The Real Housewives of Atlanta* hold peaches, I selected an ordinary onion to symbolize all of us ordinary housewives. So, why'd I pick an onion? Of course, we all know onions can make us tear up or give us bad breath, but for real, onions add flavor to everything that might ordinarily be dull and tasteless. And as a food, onions are a secret nutritional superstar that not only block cancer dramatically, but lower cholesterol, thin the blood, and ward off illness. I chose the onion because of its figurative and literal meanings. Why shouldn't the onion represent all the domestic goddesses out there raising kids and running a house, and those women who have a little gig on the side called a full-time job?

Really, I believe within every ordinary housewife there lies an extraordinary woman with a tale to tell. There are many stories that lie below the surface, somewhere between caring for and educating children, cleaning, cooking, and prioritizing their relationships and family's needs. Their secrets are much like mine, and in their reality, add up to hidden truths. Maybe that's why I love reality TV, because I see a common thread or connection to another person who is also suffering. Aren't the "real housewives" just women like us, but with better clothes? They are living with sadness and stress brought about by real life, which includes mental illness, domestic violence, depression, addictions, and a variety of personality disorders. You see, I find comfort in knowing I am not the only one to have faced these issues.

In lots of ways, writing this memoir is similar to having aired my intimate secrets on national television. I guess in a way, it's very fashionable to allow others to walk a mile in your high heels. But the one big, glaring difference is that my life is real, painfully real, not scripted. So after spending more than three years on a bathroom floor, crying uncontrollably about my health or love life, I came to the conclusion that only raw onions should make people cry.

I got up off that bathroom floor. So what, if I fell down seven times, hey, I stood up eight. And since I had nothing to hide, I decided to open up, be straight with the world, and divulge my painful past. At first, it felt taboo to share everything. I was brought up to believe all family secrets should stay within the confines of the family. Trust me, I am like most people—I really don't want every single aspect of my life publicly known. Who wants to let probing eyes see your every flaw and every mistake? Isn't that tantamount to putting yourself on the chopping block?

But no matter how hard I try, I can't keep to myself the cesspool of amoral behavior I have lived through any longer. Maybe I don't want my neighbors knowing I tried cocaine, but I do want to help them if they think they're alone in dealing with any of life's painful issues. So, instead of gossiping, I decided to become transparent— you know, easily read. Obviously, it's not all that hard to read what I am thinking or feeling. Many of you may wonder whether, had Marcus not abandoned me, would I still be with him today? Well, if I am going to honest, then the answer is yes. I would still be miserable in my marriage, because I didn't feel important enough, or love myself enough, to leave. And I mistakenly believed I could protect my kids from both husbands,

See, as long as I was willing to keep everything neat and orderly, nothing was going to change. Colon cancer was the reality check our relationship needed; I mean, there is nothing neat and orderly about the shit hitting the fan. I had to reach for hands that weren't there, time and time again during my affliction, to find out who I truly was. In the wake of my relationship explosion, I heard the voice of my brother Niall ask "Is it better to have loved and lost, than never to have loved at all?"

Those words have lingered in my head for years. Is the pain of losing someone you love, even someone who is not good for you, worth the love that you shared? Sure, we all grieve at some point for love lost, whether that loss is from a breakup or death. Well, within six months of my last divorce being finalized, I received a call from a familiar voice. I guess I wasn't the only one thinking about loss. My cell phone rang around three o'clock in the morning. It was Garrett, calling from the basement of his girlfriend's house up north. Obviously, living states away, he wasn't looking for a booty call. We hadn't spoken in quite a while, but when an ex calls you so late at night, or early in the morning, it is a pretty good indication that he's missing you.

He said, "Hey, what's up, Fiona?"

I said, "I'm sleeping. Is something wrong?"

Garrett asked if I still loved him, because he still loved me and wanted me to know I was the love of his life.

For the love of God, why did he then ask whom I loved more, him or Marcus? Call it jealousy or even male ego, but I had to squash that question down immediately. It was an impossible task to compare which of my ex-husbands I loved more and why. Oh, how I wished I told him, "You hurt me more than I deserved, because I loved you more than you deserved." I just let him speak, showering me with compliment after compliment, but oddly, I felt nothing. I guess, our past was passed, and the love we had shared had long since died. No longer did I want to maintain contact with him. That ship had sailed; yet here was my first husband, still damaged and reaching out for love.

My life had changed, I had changed, and things were different now. I get it, he was feeling regret. Who doesn't have those should-have and could-have moments and questions?

I needed to remember that this life is a test—it is only a test. I mean really, if it had been a real life, wouldn't I have been born with further instructions? So, I must constantly remind myself that this life is only a test. But thank God, life is also full of second chances. Even after Marcus had been so brutal to me while I was sick, he was given a second chance to be kind to a loved one who was hospitalized. In December 2010, my extremely abusive mother-in-law suffered a cerebral hemorrhage. Marcus had the nerve to call and blame me for the fact that a major artery had burst in his mother's brain—I mean, really, talk about projecting his guilt onto another person, right?

I remember feeling defensive, yet I said with clarity, "God is giving you a second chance to be kind to someone who is very ill. Do everything you can to support her. I know how important it is that you are there by her side!" I dug down deep, unearthing what I believe was my empathy for her suffering. Wanting to help but not impose, I sent her a basket of all the things that helped me get through my lonely days and nights in a hospital. I hoped it was the first step toward improving the future state of all our lives, but Sheryl harshly rejected my peace offering.

God forbid, on what might have been her deathbed, she could have righted some of her wrongs, atoned for some of her wrongdoings. But just like her son, she externalized blame for all the negative events in her life. As fate would have it, Dr. Eskioglu—the doctor who saved Connor's life—saved Sheryl's life. God's goodness knows no bounds; he has given her yet another chance to test the limits of her soul. For I truly believe love is not a choice, not an accident, but a decision that supports our soul's growth. Only now, I realize that the love I felt for both Garrett and Marcus wasn't healthy. I may rail against fate, but I am going to give it my all to return to being that carefree, untroubled person who existed before I met them.

There is no way I can be ashamed of my past. It has made me the woman I am today. I have had to learn to roll with the punches. And honestly, it felt as if I had been punched hard when I learned, shortly after our divorce, that Marcus and Annie got engaged at the same Ritz Carlton hotel where we did. Okay, that choice showed he lacked originality, and maybe he just had to keep pursuing the beach-walk engagement proposal of his dreams. And another bizarre fact was that Marcus married Annie, his best friend and soul mate—his words, not mine—on my birthday? Seriously, you just can't make this stuff up!

Here's another curve ball that really hit home: Marcus adopted a set of two- and four-year-old brothers. I have always believed that children come through us but don't belong to us; we are here to guide them through life as best we can.

I mean, really, what judge in his right mind allowed this psychopath to become the father of two innocent little boys? It's kind of eerie, how much these two towheaded brothers look like my boys did when Marcus and I first met. Within two years, Marcus had completely replaced his family of five with another, identical family. Talk about a weirdo!

But even though I was betrayed by the man I loved, I have come to the point of forgiveness. But that's not to say there aren't these real moments when I acknowledge the fact that Marcus is still a real A-hole, and his wife, Annie—well, mamma mia, she's still a real "bee-ach!" That said, after all I have lived through, the truth is I still wouldn't wish what happened to me on even my worst enemies. Cancer is such a hideous disease that no one, and I mean no one, really deserves to struggle with it. Add to it the fact that I was abandoned right at the moment I needed support from my life partner; that greatly multiplied the pain and sorrow. What I do remember saying to Annie—in our one and only meeting—remains true. "You'd better not get sick, really sick, or he'll leave you, too!"

So I ask myself again, was it better to have loved and lost? My answer is heck, yes; it was worth it, because under the burden of grief existed a silver lining, which was the opportunity to love myself. My journey through love, loss, and cancer has been a unique gift that cannot be exchanged, replaced, or refunded. I think I am making the most of this gift by sharing it with you, so please handle my story with care. What I wish for all women perfectly stated in Sr. Ruth Marlene Fox's prayer. I pray, God bless you with a restless discomfort about easy answers, half truths, and superficial relationships, so that you may seek truth boldly and love deep within your heart. That you, too, are also blessed with the gift of tears for those who suffer from pain and rejection or the loss of all that they cherish, so that you may reach out your hand to comfort them and transform their pain into joy! And lastly, may God bless you with enough foolishness to believe that you really can make a difference in this world, so that you are able, with God's grace, to do what others claim cannot be done.

Chapter 16:

AND THE TRUTH WILL SET YOU FREE

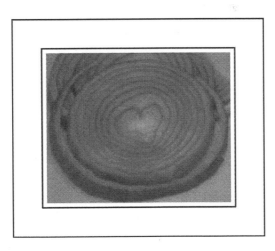

"The truth will set you free, but first it will make you miserable."
—James A. Garfield

We've all seen the commercials for those dating websites to view photos of local singles. "Go ahead! It's *free* to look!" Well, only days after the final break with Marcus, that headline caught my eye, and I signed up for a free three-day trial promotion on Match.com. I mean, it's not like I was ready to date. My relationship was over, but I wasn't over it, and I was still incredibly ill. Honestly, I think I was just curious to see what was out there, with no real intention of looking for love. Because I submitted my e-mail address, within twenty-four hours I received an e-mail back with that day's most compatible matches. Can you imagine my surprise when I opened that e-mail to discover Marcus's picture labeled as a 98 percent match to me? You gotta be kidding me. I burst into tears. Obviously my soon-to-be ex-husband wasn't allowing any grass to grow under his wiener. Of course, I was shocked, even if I too was there online, I wasn't really fishing! What about Annie, Penny, and God only knows who else? It was just another sign from above that Marcus was not and never had been the man for me.

Not long after the divorce, I was able to visit friends—Lisa and Brandon—a married couple who had been friends with both my ex and me for years. While we were enjoying a glass of wine, our conversation took an unexpected turn. Brandon leaned into my personal space and said, "I love the fullness of your lips and would really like to kiss you now." What? Was I dreaming? He continued to compliment me. I looked toward Lisa for help. She smiled sweetly and said, "We've had sex with other women, Fiona." What the heck…Did she just say *we*? No way. My mind went into overload. I wondered how long to just sit there, before I could get up without them knowing I was extremely uncomfortable with their proposal.

I wasn't upset with Brandon—or with Lisa, for that matter. They lived their lives on their terms and didn't make any excuses for that. Brandon tried to sway me by telling me he'd be happy to call Marcus afterward and let him know what a good lover I am.

"Oh Jesus," I told him, "that would only make matters worse for me." They asked what I wanted—you know, my type of guy? And if I wanted they could maybe set me up with their attractive Latino neighbor, but only if I was ready to jump right back in the saddle.

But since I happened to be a serial monogamist, I just couldn't accept any of their kind offers. Years have passed, and apparently my sex life resembles tumbleweed rolling across a deserted frontier town. I miss having fun, you know, those Wild, Wild West days. Well, okay, maybe they weren't always that wild. But in any case, I just don't want to get ambushed by any more bandits. I had to leave the shoot-'em-up frontier boomtown and wait till the gun smoke cleared.

I know three years is a long time to be celibate, but I had been divorced twice, and for my sake, I needed to learn why that occurred. And it took time, lots and lots of time. Abstaining from sex sucks. But most days it took a lot of effort to simply get up, take a shower, get dressed—you know, continue with my everyday life. But God knows, I needed to take time for me and the children.

Around the one-year mark after the divorce, I caved in and decided to give online dating a real shot. There were just so many dating sites to choose from: Match. com, Plenty of Fish, Zoosk, eHarmony, and even religious dating sites like Christian Mingle. Most dating sites demand a membership fee, but there are a couple of sites that are 100 percent free. Actually, I found the price of those free sites is one's sanity. I experienced the difference in the kinds of people you meet on free or paid dating websites: you get what you pay for.

Honestly, I found the experience of online dating hilarious, and so I can't help but want to dish on all the different types of men I met online. It truly was enough to keep me single. I'll be the first to agree with the statement that "a picture is worth a thousand words," especially when it comes to Internet dating. What's up with all the men holding fish as their main profile picture? I've got nothing against fishing, but what I would find sexier is if there were more photos of these single guys doing the laundry, grocery shopping, or hand-washing the dishes. Those photos would be priceless!

I learned quickly about all the different types of men available today online. There was the fast-moving guy who was discussing us living together after two dates, the no-photo guy who loved my picture but refused to send his, and the family guy who includes his kids in his profile picture. I imagine that tactic makes an ex-wife or two pretty angry. Of course I met the liar guy who understated his height, weight, or reason for wanting to meet. Within five seconds to five minutes I knew he wasn't slender or athletic and toned, nor was he six feet tall, and it wasn't a long-term relationship that he had on his mind.

Between the newly "separated" men and the sugar daddies, I really didn't find what I was looking for online. But I highly recommend the experience, if only for the laughs. And I suggest that you enjoy a glass of wine or two on your dates. Chelsea Handler knows what she's talking about: *"When a guy tells me I don't need a drink to make myself more fun to be around, I tell him, 'I'm drinking so that you're more fun to be around.'"* Trust me, you're lucky if your date buys your drink, coffee, or dinner. One date wanted to share a dinner, saying it was "more intimate," but I thought, *Cheapo!*

And oh my God, after a friend and I swapped stories about our recent dates, we discovered we each went on a date, a week apart, with the same guy. Talk about a small town! With that said, there was also the time Match. com sent my brother Niall my photograph and bio in his compatible daily matches. Creepy. Honestly, Match.com should be called Matchless.com. At least I had a few fun times, hangin' with twenty- and thirty-somethings who were seriously SMEXY—smart and sexy.

Well, you've guessed it by now; I have yet to meet the man of my dreams. But if the truth be known, I was just playing at dating. What I mean to say is, after I've been hit on by my family priest, a couple wanting a ménage à trois, a married man into swinging, and one, okay, maybe two women, can you blame me for being a little gun-shy with regard to getting back in the saddle?

There was no way I could continue online dating, or look to enter a loving relationship, until I loved myself. I also needed lose my naïve fantasies and yearnings for a perfect love. If I was ever going to find love I need to search for the truth about my life.

"Then you will know the truth, and the truth will set you free" (John 8:32). Really, it was much easier to survive cancer than to confront my shadow after surviving the relationship with Marcus. I had to accept that God answered my call to save my life, and in exchange he took Marcus, because he doesn't give us the people we

want. He gives us the people we need. Finally, I came to terms with the fact that people come into our lives for a reason, a season, or a lifetime. And although the season of our lives together has passed, Marcus still haunts my dreams in one recurring memory. Honestly, it's more like a recurring nightmare, or flashback, of the last time we were intimate.

Some nights, I awake, traumatized after re-experiencing the last sexual encounter with Marcus, and since I can't get the thought out of my mind, I'll share it, in hopes of setting the truth free. Truthfully, never in a million years did I—an ordinary wife and mother—think I would share details of my sex life. But here goes. Almost three years ago, on a warm fall evening, I arrived at my husband's newly renovated condominium. Separated for months, I desperately wanted to rekindle our relationship. I knew my husband still found me attractive, so earlier that afternoon I had purchased a royal-blue lace-up corset, black panties, and thigh-high sheer stockings. The scene was set for unforgettable sex—the lights were dim, candles lit, and even soft background music was playing.

Truly, I just wanted to bask in the warmth of my husband's arms and feel his love again. Marcus had always believed himself to be sensual, even seductive. Without a doubt he believed he could satisfy any woman, yet for most of our relationship, he just couldn't satisfy me in bed. For thirteen years, the sex I had experienced with Marcus was all about power and control. But that particular night, I didn't care, I wanted to dress up and be there for him, while trying to just accept him for who he was, the man whom I still loved.

Marcus purred in his sexiest voice to hurry, he was becoming impatient. He smiled approvingly as he watched me walk toward him. My hair was ruffled, my outfit was far from prim and proper, and my skin glowed under the soft lighting. Marcus pulled me toward him on the bed, quickly unleashing the lace from the corset. He then leaned back, stared at my scar, and said, "Hey, baby, don't worry. Someday, someone, somewhere, won't mind having you with that scar." I couldn't focus, as his hurtful words just hung there in the air, while he began kissing my entire body.

I tried to make eye contact with my spouse, but he either looked away or closed his eyes. It was draining

I guess it was just another power play to deliberately not give me what I so craved: real intimacy. And then, just then, I heard the words I had been waiting to hear throughout my entire illness. Marcus whispered, "I love you" in my ear, as he slid his arm around the small of my back. But the very moment those precious words slipped from his mouth, he winced. Can you believe it? He drew back from me, and his entire body tensed up as if he was in real pain. And then there was that expression on his face that showed distress as he inhaled a rather large breath of air. It was like he was trying to suck back the words that I needed to hear!

I know he said those words, but I will never really know if he meant them. Maybe it was a knee-jerk reaction to the passionate sex. But his attempt to take back his words left me feeling not very good about myself. No matter how sweet or sexy I was, for Marcus sex was a mechanical act, and I was a mere object. He couldn't become emotional. He was reveling in the act of sex; you could hardly call it lovemaking. And in Marcus's world, intimacy and commitment did not exist. I didn't know at the time that this night was to be our last night together. I was just a sexual conquest—great sex, nonetheless—but I never wanted to play his head games. Although I must commend him on his ability to morph into whatever others desire, I ultimately wanted to get beyond his surface veneer.

We had a lot of the ingredients that go into making successful and memorable sex. But sadly, my costar was emotionless, manipulative, and yes, calculating. I know I'm not the only woman who wants a much higher level of oneness with the man she loves. It's not as if there isn't a time and place for just the physical act of fucking. But what if you find out that's all you ever had with the man you spent your life with? I was just a means to boosting my husband's ego, and once he felt he had me, really had me, he didn't want me anymore, because he felt he had "won" the game, the game of love.

But what sealed the deal in knowing that something was innately wrong with Marcus happened after the sex. His true colors really showed through after I returned to the bedroom from using the restroom. Unfortunately, our passionate encounter left Marcus feeling victorious. He was reveling in the fact he had secured my love, again.

It was a shocking thing to hear Marcus laughing like a hyena, while lying nude on the bed. If you could have only seen him from my perspective, with his ankles up, tucked behind his ears, facing me. Now, is the time he gives me eye contact? Really? His hands reached around as if he were a contortionist. He grabbed his ass and pulled his cheeks apart, allowing me to witness his vulgarity. Yes, ma'am, that asshole was showing me his asshole!

He was acting on his impulse and desire and didn't care about social conventions. Not only did I find him disgusting, but I realized that I was crazy to think that I could connect as one with this man. He was far more interested in debasing his and my dignity! I guess he had no real self to bring to our relationship. So instead of showing me that he loved me, he wanted to shock me and feel powerful by being sexually explicit. I was reminded again that Marcus didn't hold anyone or anything sacred. What he valued was degradation and devaluation, making me feel unworthy, inadequate, and yes, even subhuman.

I believed the devil had left hell and had taken the form of my enticing husband. For it has been said that the devil must be a handsome man, not ugly and frightening. Why else would people find him so attractive? It's not like Marcus had any emotional competency. It really was a miracle we weren't torn apart sooner. While it's not as if I was able to turn off my feelings like a switch, after this final experience with Marcus I knew we could never have a truly loving relationship.

My love for my ex-husband enslaved me for years, but now, finally, I am free. God only knows why I cried for so long over someone who couldn't love me back. You really gotta love Eleanor Roosevelt, who said, *"We are afraid to care too much, for fear that the other person does not care at all."* It is only now that I can admit to being ready to "feel" the presence of real love. I believe my mind keeps replaying this last horrible memory to remind me that Marcus can't give or receive love. This truth helped set me free. And in my quest to heal my life, I hope I can help empower others to search for their truth.

Martin Luther King's hope was that people would be judged… *"by the content of their character."* A reputation grows out of good character, but if it is built on lies, then it is like a house built with playing cards—it's bound to fall! My biggest lesson learned thus far was that suffering produces perseverance, character, and above all, hope. Everything around me collapsed, and with time I learned to rejoice in my suffering while allowing my persistence and tenacity to shine through.

No matter what life throws at us, we each have the power to choose to learn from our experiences. This is the single force that shapes the quality of our lives.

An Original Poem
by the Author

Listen girls, once upon a time
There was a girl who loved to rhyme.
No fairy tale her life would be.

The girl grew up; she's mom to three.
Her heart was broken, you'll see,
Diagnosed with cancer—stage three!

Crushed by him who proposed on knee,
He abused her and then did flee.
Love yourself to a higher degree!

Difficult, she won't disagree,
To heal, she uncovered the key:
Her own pure thoughts
helped set her free.

Being perfect maybe okay for Barbie.
But just remember she ended up with a guy
with plastic balls.
—Unknown Author

Request to All the Readers of *Raw*

You know, God gave us a pinky finger just to make pinky promises with our friends. After all I have shared, I consider you a friend, so I am asking you to swear you'll take a few moments of your life and write a review of this book on Amazon.com. Of course, I want you to write an honest review; whatever opinion you wish to share will be appreciated. Don't forget to check out my website: www.fiona-finn.com and remember, never break a pinky promise!

88804356R00141

Made in the USA
Columbia, SC
04 February 2018